Teaching through Challenges for Equity, Diversity, and Inclusion (EDI)

Teaching through Challenges for Equity, Diversity, and Inclusion (EDI)

Stephanie L. Burrell Storms,
Sarah K. Donovan, and
Theodora P. Williams

ROWMAN & LITTLEFIELD
Lanham • Boulder • New York • London

Published by Rowman & Littlefield
An imprint of The Rowman & Littlefield Publishing Group, Inc.
4501 Forbes Boulevard, Suite 200, Lanham, Maryland 20706
www.rowman.com

6 Tinworth Street, London SE11 5AL, United Kingdom

British Library Cataloguing in Publication Information Available

Library of Congress Cataloging-in-Publication Data

Names: Burrell Storms, Stephanie L., author. | Donovan, Sarah K., 1973- author. | Williams, Theodora P., 1944- author.
Title: Teaching through challenges for equity, diversity, and inclusion (EDI) / Stephanie L. Burrell Storms, Sarah K. Donovan, and Theodora P. Williams.
Description: Lanham : Rowman & Littlefield Publishers, [2020] | Includes bibliographical references.
Identifiers: LCCN 2019050354 (print) | LCCN 2019050355 (ebook) | ISBN 9781475843385 (cloth) | ISBN 9781475843392 (paperback) | ISBN 9781475843408 (epub)
Subjects: LCSH: Multicultural education—Study and teaching. | Educational equalization. | Inclusive education—Study and teaching.
Classification: LCC LC1099 .B87 2020 (print) | LCC LC1099 (ebook) | DDC 379.2/6—dc23
LC record available at https://lccn.loc.gov/2019050354
LC ebook record available at https://lccn.loc.gov/2019050355

Contents

PART III: TECHNOLOGY AND SOCIAL ACTION

PART IV: AFFECTIVE CONSIDERATIONS

PART V: REFLECTION FOR CRITICAL CONSCIOUSNESS

PART VI: SAFE SPACES AND RESISTANCE

Foreword

Betty J. Overton

Equity, diversity, and inclusion (EDI): During the last twenty years, few terms in higher education have provoked more explosive rhetoric or fevered goal setting and planning. But the progress from rhetoric to action has been slow and often contested. Institutions adopt EDI almost like a mantra, yet many persons within institutions and outside are still uncertain about what the term really means or the steps needed to turn discussions and good intentions into action. This is not because of a lack of evidence about the benefits of EDI.

Research (Clayton-Pedersen, 2007; Pope, 2009; Williams, 2013) is increasingly providing testimony that institutional efforts that prioritize equity, diversity, and inclusion create learning environments that respect and value individual differences across varying dimensions (e.g., race, gender, socio-economic, age, sexual orientation, and other areas), and the historical evidence of the educational benefits of diversity have been reinforced over time.

But when we are honest about our ability to increase diversity, to support equity, and to achieve genuine inclusion, we have to acknowledge that our efforts have not always translated into progress on campuses, created community environments that enable people of different backgrounds to succeed, or fostered mission-advancing EDI perspectives to be embraced at our institutions.

Despite the assertion of a reality I see far too often, there is also good news. The EDI work is going forward, and there is a growing cadre of people willing to be engaged in it. The group includes many early-career faculty and administrators. This dedicated and mission-driven community of scholar-teachers is adamant about change, and they are ready to move our institutions. What they need is a continuous infusion of ideas, honest talk about challenges and strategies, and good companions on the journey. And that is what this companion text to the first EDI volume, *Breaking Down Silos for Equity, Diversity, and Inclusion (EDI)*, delivers.

The editors of this volume focused the publication on the core of our business—the classroom. *Teaching through Challenges for Equity, Diversity, and Inclusion* joins other books about diversity in the classroom in echoing the message that inclusive classrooms foster learning and minimize bias. These EDI classrooms recognize and address systemic inequities, which create disadvantages for students, but also impact faculty, administrators, and staff. Attention to these inequities in the learning experience is about social justice but also about institutional effectiveness.

It is important that these issues are being reinforced in this publication. However, what makes this offering a welcome and refreshing departure from past volumes is its use of the larger framework of equity, diversity, and inclusion, signaling a broader perspective and approach to thinking about classroom practice.

Embedded in the chapters is a consideration that diversity in and of itself is not sufficient to create the types of comprehensive change our classrooms need. These authors understand that diversity without inclusion creates isolation, marginality, and resentment among those "let in," and diversity without equity builds new caste systems of the haves and have-nots. Therefore, the authors have tackled complex inclusion issues such as how we create new habits of mind as we prepare future teachers for whom the idea of EDI must be second nature.

They raise equity questions about handling affective issues such as naming privilege and shame in the classroom, or embodied learning through mindfulness, and how these can be beneficial to all aspects of EDI. They rethink "safe spaces," resistance to discussions about EDI for a diverse student body, and how building cross-disciplinary course assignments can result in social action outcomes. They tackle how inclusion and exclusion function within equity, diversity, and inclusion. There is much in the chapters to chew on as contributors dig deep into essential questions and issues to illuminate new pathways to learning for our students and breakthroughs in our understanding of how EDI operates within pedagogical strategies.

Like its companion edition (*Breaking Down Silos*), *Teaching through Challenges* takes an interdisciplinary approach, interested in proven examples and useful lessons. The chapters are well curated to highlight efforts grounded in sound scholarship and practice borne of experimentation through trial, error, and evolving success. This book might be especially helpful to educators interested in learning about what it takes to initiate EDI work, develop strong programs, and sustain them. Administrators will find it useful as an overview of the types of faculty-generated activities that are yielding results and might be encouraged or incentivized on their campuses.

In focusing on the classroom, and the challenges educators will encounter, this book places EDI at the core of the work of higher education. It is the place where EDI sometimes has the hardest chance of getting a foothold, but it is also the place where higher education can promote equity and civil discourse. Therefore, we should all welcome this new resource pushing us forward.

Betty J. Overton
National Forum on Higher Education for the Public Good
University of Michigan

REFERENCES

Clayton-Pedersen, A. R., Parker, S., Smith, D. G., Moreno, J. F., and Teraguchi, D. H. (2007). Making a real difference with diversity: A guide to institutional change. Washington, DC: Association of American Colleges and Universities.

Pope, R. L., Mueller, J. A., and Reynolds, A. L. (2009). Looking back and moving forward: Future directions for diversity research in student affairs. *Journal of College Student Development*, 50(6), 640–58.

Williams, D. A. (2013). *Strategic diversity leadership: Activating change and transformation in higher education.* Sterling, VA: Stylus Publishing.

Preface

Stephanie L. Burrell Storms, Sarah K. Donovan, and Theodora P. Williams

Twenty-first-century educators cannot ignore the increasingly diverse student population in their classrooms and the value of student intercultural awareness in competitive job markets. However, higher education moves at a slower pace than the world outside. While educators may be aware of a need to understand equity, diversity, and inclusion (EDI) goals in relationship to their disciplines, and institutions may support EDI in theory, the onus of pedagogical training in EDI often falls on individual educators motivated to seek out their own resources.

In the summer of 2016, the authors of this edited volume explored issues such as these in a Faculty Resource Network seminar on EDI at New York University. What began as open and honest conversations about EDI developed first into a cross-discipline collaboration—and ultimately a published article—between six conference participants (Hartwell et al., 2017), and then into an expanded project across more disciplines in this book and its companion text, *Breaking Down Silos for Equity, Diversity, and Inclusion.*

This book and its companion text are written by faculty and administrators for educators who value the goals of EDI and seek an intellectual community to help them develop their practice. While both texts offer strategies and activities for the classroom, this text takes as its starting point the challenges of teaching with EDI goals.

Included in this book are chapters from a range of educators, including social justice education experts and also educators who have taught themselves how to incorporate EDI goals into their classroom. Foremost in this book is an honest discussion of common challenges faculty may face when they engage in this difficult work, along with effective strategies for addressing them. While intended as practical guides to educators, these chapters have another goal: to encourage reflection within higher education as a whole with regard to the value of institutionalizing EDI goals so that educators have pedagogical support when challenges arise.

REFERENCES

Hartwell, E., Cole, K., Donohue, S., Greene, R., Burrell Storms, S., and Williams, T. (2017). Breaking down silos: Teaching equity, diversity, and inclusion across the disciplines, *Humboldt Journal of Social Relations*, 1(39), 143–62.

Introduction

Stephanie L. Burrell Storms, Sarah K. Donovan, and Theodora P. Williams

In *Teaching through Challenges for Equity, Diversity, and Inclusion*, chapters are grouped according to six different themes: respect for divergent learning styles; inclusion and exclusion; technology and social action; affective considerations; reflection for critical consciousness; and safe spaces and resistance.

Chapters one and two address respect for divergent learning styles. Kim, in chapter one, discusses how to challenge and dismantle the persistent negative conceptualization of disability in education to promote equity, diversity, and inclusion (EDI) for all. While this chapter pertains, in particular, to pedagogical strategies used in the classroom with future teachers, it also contains activities and habits of mind that may be useful to educators across the disciplines to challenge existing biases about ability in higher education.

In chapter two, Kraft and Hermberg address the current climate in higher education for students with divergent learning styles and disabilities. Underscoring the narrow range of institutional accommodations in higher education, as compared to K-12, they examine the changes that individual instructors can make—beyond accommodation—to create a positive learning environment for all students.

Chapters three and four discuss the topics of inclusion and exclusion with regard to EDI. In chapter three, Miller discusses how it has become mainstream to critique dominant discourse in higher education but points out that these critiques often neglect the experience of American Indians and American Indian tribes. Central to this experience is the concept of sovereignty and indigeneity. Miller examines how both are often contradictory to the narrative of diversity as a melting pot. She proposes lesson plans for integrating sovereignty into the higher education curriculum.

Garcia, McCoy, and Nguyen introduce and utilize, in chapter four, the paradox of inclusion/exclusion to frame and address the challenges they face with their EDI goals in the classroom. In particular, they underscore the tension that all educators experience as they navigate which issues and theories to include in the classroom and the necessity of excluding ideas that may threaten the very culture of EDI.

Burrell Storms, Rozgonyi, and Rainville, the authors of chapter five, and Bowen in chapter six address and explore the relationship between technology and social action. Burrell Storms, Rozgonyi, and Rainville describe how a collaboration across two disciplines—social justice education (SJE) and educational technology (EdTech)—engaged students enrolled in the SJE course in a social action project to create public service announcements that promoted EDI. As they describe the project, the authors point to its broader applicability across disciplines.

Bowen examines how an English course on literacy and language can advance EDI through a combination of archival research with Federal Writers' Project interviews and community engagement. Bowen describes how students learned about historical and contemporary structural forces that affect literacy and acted on that knowledge by serving as tutors at a community elementary school. She also addresses how this combination of archival research and community engagement is transferable to other disciplines.

Chapters seven, eight, and nine engage with affective considerations, such as embodied learning and processing affects, within the classroom. In chapter seven, Forrest and Thompson discuss the relationship between shame and EDI work in the classroom. They discuss the value of increasing students' awareness of how shame is self-operating in the classroom and in society to perpetuate patterns of privilege and oppression. They provide an overview and examples of what working with shame looks like in the classroom.

Gill-Lopez, in chapter eight, describes how teachers and students in higher education can practice mindfulness to bring to light their own implicit biases. The first section defines mindfulness and implicit bias, and it describes their points of intersection using a neuroscience lens. The second section describes specific mindful awareness practices (MAPS) that can be used by EDI instructors and students to enhance their own self-awareness, knowledge, skill, and behavior in the classroom.

In chapter nine, Wong and Hilario introduce readers to the Acceptance and Commitment to Empowerment (ACE) approach to transformative learning. They illustrate a selected application of ACE-based learning principles and activities to promote dialogue, reflexivity, and commitment toward social justice, equity, diversity, and inclusion among university students in nursing and allied health/social care disciplines.

Bergstrom, in chapter ten, and Morrison, in chapter eleven, discuss reflection as a way to enhance critical consciousness. Bergstrom describes how the Intercultural Development Inventory (IDI) is employed in an online course sequence to guide students through a process of reflection and action with regard to their intercultural understanding. She documents how sustained engagement with the IDI—through a pre-test, capstone project, and post-test—results in measurable gains for EDI goals.

Morrison discusses person-centered teaching and learning goals as a means of encouraging self-reflection in students that is crucial for those who wish to be advocates in any field. After a brief introduction to the person-centered approach, and its roots in social justice education and advocacy, the chapter examines the different goals that comprise the approach, sample assignments or activities, and their connection to EDI.

Chapters twelve and thirteen rethink safe spaces and resistance. In chapter twelve, Barber draws on years of experience facilitating workshops about race with diverse groups of students across the United States, naming four typical points of resistance in discussions about EDI. As she employs illustrative examples to describe these resistances, she also indicates strategies that will help educators address each one.

Adamo, in chapter thirteen, characterizes the current student perspective in higher education regarding speech on campus and draws out different meanings and expectations about "safe spaces" in higher education. Adamo then offers recommendations for how instructors might establish and manage maximally inclusive dialogue in their classrooms so that they can achieve social justice and EDI goals and create a respectful environment in which students can learn.

While all of the chapters address EDI challenges that instructors might encounter in a higher education classroom with specific disciplines or professional contexts in mind, the strategies, activities, and insights are broadly applicable across disciplines and institutions.

The goal of writing about these broad issues is to emphasize that educators should move beyond identifying EDI goals and challenges as belonging to select specializations such as sociology or education. If EDI goals are within the purview of all disciplines that serve the twenty-first-century student, then educators can benefit from open discussion of the challenges, strategies, and practices to approach them.

Part I

RESPECT FOR DIVERGENT
LEARNING STYLES

Chapter One

Placing ~~dis~~Ability Front and Center in EDI Studies

Hyun Uk Kim

It was the enactment of the Education for All Handicapped Children (EHA) Act (Public Law 94-142, now known as the Individuals with Disabilities Education Improvement [IDEA] Act) in 1975 that guaranteed the right to a free and appropriate public education (FAPE) for all children and youth between the ages of three to twenty-one with disability labels. Subsequently, colleges and universities are subject to the Americans with Disabilities Act (ADA), Section 504 of the Rehabilitation Act of 1973, or both, in order to provide nondiscrimination protection against anyone based on the disability.

Despite these federal mandates and protection, these students are less likely to go to and complete college (Sanford et al., 2011). While college and university brochures and websites depict people of different races and ethnicities, if and when students with disabilities are portrayed on college and university brochures and websites, they are typically depicted only on the pages of accommodations and disability services (Davis, 2011).

The purpose of this chapter is to share how to challenge and to dismantle the persistent negative conceptualization of disability so as to promote equity, diversity, and inclusion for all through pedagogical strategies useful not only for teacher educators but also for faculty across the disciplines. This chapter works within a social model of disability that challenges a deficit model. After a brief introduction to the social model, it explores six strategies that matter: reading, history, instructional design, direct contact, inclusion, and labels.

Students are often introduced to the field of special education through textbooks that follow a deficit model. The books are written by people without any disabilities whose terminal degree is in special education. These authors often compartmentalize special education and disability in discrete disability categories, from their "disabling" characteristics to disability-specific

teaching strategies, based on what they have learned about people with disability labels.

With this instructional approach, disability is thought to be nothing but
internal to the person with a given disability label. There are, then, specific
teaching strategies pertaining to each disability category that each student
needs to be successful in schools and strategies that teachers must master to
teach them well. This particular way of conceptualizing disability is referred
to as the "deficit model" or "medical model" of disability. It constructs disability as a problem that resides in an individual in desperate need of intervention and remediation.

Alternatively, the social model of disability, coined by Mike Oliver in
1983, contextualizes disability within political and social spheres and contends that people are disabled not by their bodies but by society (Oliver, 1990;
UPIAS, 1976). Disability Studies in Education (DSE), a discipline within the
broader framework of the social model of disability, provides

> a counterbalance to the deficit-based understanding of disability that permeates
> education as how we choose to respond to disability shifts significantly depend-
> ing upon whether we perceive that something is "wrong" with disabled people
> or something is "wrong" with a social system that disables people (Valle and
> Connor, 2011, p. xi).

The following strategies work within the social model of disability.

READING MATTERS

Professors can make choices in their selections of readings that challenge the
deficit model. Instead of using or assigning textbooks compartmentalized by
disability types imbued in the deficit model, first-person accounts of living
and having a disability can be introduced so that students learn from them,
not just about them.

For example, in an introductory special education course, one strategy to
challenge the deficit model is for students to read a book written by a person
with a disability label.[1] In this assignment, either a book title chosen by students or assigned by a faculty member empowers students to become empathetic, not sympathetic, toward people with a disability label so as to establish
genuine respect and high expectations through meaningful relationships with
people with a disability label (Nieto, 2006).

Another strategy is to read about how disability is constructed in other
cultures. The Hmong, for example, often believe that people with epilepsy,

or *quag dab peg*, see things that others cannot, and that they can more easily enter a trance to journey to the spirit world, hence *quag dab peg*, which literally means "the spirit catches you and you fall down" (Fadiman, 1997). Similarly, the Navajo culture lacked a word for "disability," as a person's condition is seen as part of one's personality (Kapp, 2011).

In their article "What Lula Lacks," two anthropologists, Haldane and Crawford (2010), share how Lula, their daughter with autism, becomes "comprehensible, engaged, wholly human" (p. 26) among Moroccan children.

These readings can be incorporated into a course in any discipline to show that knowledge and learning can be both cultural and perspectival. Diversifying reading materials, from books and articles[2] written by people with a disability label to those written about different cultures on disability,[3] can help acknowledge and combat the danger of a single story (see Adichie, 2009).

HISTORY MATTERS

Another pedagogical strategy is to have students research the social and historical contexts for a given disability label and learn how they have evolved. This can be utilized as an activity to illustrate intersectionality and privilege between (dis)ability and other identities, as in Crenshaw (1989) about race and sex and in McIntosh about white privilege (1989).

Historically, people with disability labels in the United States were perceived as possessed by the devil until the 1700s, genetically defective in the 1940s, unfortunate and pitiful in the 1970s, and as competent, independent, and self-determined in the 2000s (Adams, Bell, and Griffin, 2007). The latter perspective has emerged by the self-organization of people with a disability label (Charlton, 1998). Disability has been understood as a human rights issue over the latter half of the twentieth century (Rioux and Carbert, 2003) because people with disabilities are among the most marginalized groups in the world (World Health Organization, 2017).

To critically examine the historical treatment toward people with disability labels as well as other groups of people who have been marginalized, students can explore how the societal perspectives and historical treatment toward these people have evolved and how the advocacy movement has helped advance the education and civil rights for all.

The knowledge and understanding of the historical treatments toward marginalized people will empower students to acknowledge the past; appreciate and challenge current trends, political issues, legislation, and litigation; and to plan for the future, with everyone in mind.

INSTRUCTIONAL DESIGN MATTERS

Diversifying contents of a course must accompany innovative and effective pedagogical approaches. One evidence-informed teaching and learning framework is Universal Design for Learning (UDL). According to CAST (n.d.), UDL is an educational framework and a set of principles to optimize teaching and to maximize learning opportunities for diverse student populations with different learning needs and styles.

In addition, UDL is designed to reduce or eliminate instructional, attitudinal, and physical barriers to students' learning. With a variety of learning formats to choose from, flexible assessments, and multiple means of demonstrating what they have learned, instructors are improving accessibility not only to learning opportunities but also increasing student success.

Professors can provide an array of reading materials in diverse formats. To use the introductory special education course as an example, readings on disability can vary from traditional textbook chapters and audiobooks to websites and personal blogs. It is imperative for professors to reflect on their own personal biases and attitudinal barriers in selecting reading materials.

Followed by intentional selections of reading materials, students are given an option to choose a format that suits them best to access their learning. Moreover, writing assignments can be diversified. Students can "write" in a different format, such as an illustration, a poem, a four-to-five-minute video, or an activity to capture and show what they have learned from the assigned readings.

Providing diverse options to demonstrate knowledge allows students to become less anxious and freer to share their ideas and takeaway from any given assignments. A professor from any discipline can allow for multiple ways to demonstrate knowledge.

UDL principles can also be applied in this by pairing up students with different learning needs and styles. Through purposeful and intentional pairing by the professor, students can learn not only from one another but about one another: Professors are creating a learning environment for students to be successful through improving how they approach teaching, not how students learn and who they are.

This type of teaching and learning can make both the instructor and the students feel uneasy because of the uncertainty it creates. However, solidifying good teaching and learning through knowledge, diversity, and inclusion is not enough unless professors assume their role as a change agent because "teaching is always about power . . . and . . . about social justice" (Nieto, 2006, p. 469).

DIRECT CONTACT MATTERS

As people with a disability label and researchers from the social and health sciences have identified the social and environmental barriers that disable people, disability has been thought of as "a distinct form of diversity in its variability, contingency, and fluidity" (Couser, 2005, p. 602). This is because anyone can become disabled, at any time, and, barring sudden or accidental death, eventually, most people will become disabled to a significant degree with age.

Connor and Bejoian (2007) further contend that negative depictions of people with disability labels must be challenged, reframed, and replaced by an understanding of disability as part of human diversity.

An effective strategy to illustrate disability as a form of diversity is by learning with and from individuals with an acquired disability label as well as with a congenital disability. For instance, people with a disability label and/or family members of those that do can be invited to the classroom as guest speakers or be interviewed in a more private, less-intimidating space for the interviewee and the interviewer.

To facilitate direct human contact, students can spend a day or two with a person with a disability label or his/her/their caregiver. These direct personal-contact opportunities can help build further empathy for, and solidarity with, people with a disability label and family members. This is particularly important because empathic people are more likely to understand and appreciate the perspectives of others, which leads to less prejudice, more positive social overtures (Feshbach and Feshbach, 2009), and less stigma and discrimination (Thornicroft, Brohan, Kassam, and Lewis-Holmes, 2008).

INCLUSION MATTERS

Sapon-Shevin (2003) posits that "when one student is not a full participant in his or her school community, then we are all at risk. By embracing inclusion as a model of social justice, we can create a world fit for us all" (p. 28). To embrace inclusion as a social justice issue (Artiles, Harris-Murri, and Rostenberg, 2006) and as a moral imperative (Balieri and Knopf, 2004), what must be acknowledged is the opposite: exclusion.

For instance, students can survey their colleges or neighborhood to assess everyday barriers and accessibility features, take a tour of familiar places with a person with a disability label, or attend or watch a sporting event that features professional athletes with a disability label, to name a few (see Baglieri and Shapiro, 2017, for a complete list). Not only do these experiential activities develop awareness about physical exclusion, but they also promote inclusion as a social justice issue.

LABELS MATTER

According to Dudley-Marling (2004), "learning and learning problems do not reside in people's heads as much as in the complex social interactions performed in a place called school that is itself situated in a broader social, political, and cultural context" (p. 483). Since the mid-1990s, there have been movements for paradigm shifts.

For instance, counseling psychologists adapted the strength-based model, focusing on an individual's assets, rather than the deficit-based model, focusing on his or her pathology (Smith, 2006). Similarly, activists with autism spectrum disorders (ASD) coined the term "neurodiversity," redefining their identity (Blume, 1998; Singer, 1999) as "differently wired" individuals, which has spread to other disability labels, such as learning disabilities, emotional and behavioral disorders, and attention deficit hyperactivity disorder (ADHD) (Hendrickx, 2010; Pollak, 2009).

Armstrong (2012) contends that neurodiversity-inspired educators have a deep respect for student differences and seek ways to create the best learning environments for all students. Similarly, neurodiversity-inspired people will also respect individual differences and seek to create equitable environments for all. This paradigm shift, for instance, can be implemented in any classroom by focusing on what students can do rather than what they cannot do (Rentenbach, Prislovsky, and Gabriel, 2017). These strength-based strategies embrace disability as different learning needs through diverse instructional strategies.

CONCLUSION

This chapter discussed different teaching and learning strategies for students and instructors to be pedagogically and psychologically competent so that everyone is empowered to promote equity, diversity, and inclusion in classrooms and in society.

To truly effect change and challenge the status quo, it is absolutely imperative that more educators and administrators in higher education institutions put ability front and center in EDI and in their respective programs, schools, and institutions. They must make fearless choices and brave decisions about inequity, injustice, and exclusion because our collective "choices, decisions, and actions transform challenges into exploration, risk into reward, and fear into determination" (Daskal, n.d.). This will help us to create a more just and inclusive society for all.

NOTES

1. A few suggested book titles include *Brilliant Imperfection* (Clare, 2017); *Songs of the Gorilla Nation* (Prince-Hughes, 2005); *The Reason I Jump: The Inner Voice of a Thirteen-Year-Old Boy with Autism* (Higashida, 2016); *The Center Cannot Hold* (Saks, 2008); and *Front of the Class: How Tourette Syndrome Made Me the Teacher I Never Had* (Cohen, 2008).

2. *Presume Competence* (Biklen and Burke, 2006); An exceptional path: An ethnographic narrative reflecting on autistic parenthood from evolutionary, cultural, and spiritual perspectives (Eddings Prince, 2010); The madwoman in the academy, or, revealing the invisible straightjacket: Theorizing and teaching saneism and same privilege (Wolframe, 2013).

3. Growing up deaf on the Vineyard (Groce, 1985); Canfei to canjo: The freedom of being loud (Ho, 2018); What Lula lacks (Haldane and Crawford, 2010); Culture and disability: Providing culturally competent services (Stone, 2005).

REFERENCES

Adams, M., Bell, L. A., and Griffin, P. (2007). (Eds.). *Teaching for diversity and social justice* (2nd ed.). New York: Routledge.

Adichie, C. N. (2009). The danger of a single story [Video file]. Retrieved from https://www.ted.com/talks/chimamanda_adichie_the_danger_of_a_single_story ?language=en.

Armstrong, T. (October, 2012). First, discover their strengths. *Educational Leadership*, 10–16.

Artiles, A. J., Harris-Murri, N., and Rostenberg, D. (2006). Inclusion as social justice: Critical notes on discourse, assumptions, and the road ahead. *Theory into Practice*, 45(3), 260–68.

Baglieri, S., and Knopf, J. H. (2004). Normalizing difference in inclusive teaching. *Journal of Learning Disabilities*, 37(6), 525–529. https://doi.org/10.1177/002221 94040370060701

Baglieri, S., and Shapiro, A. (2017). *Disability studies and the inclusive classroom: Critical practices for creating least restrictive attitudes*. New York: Routledge.

Biklen, D., and Burke, J. (2006). Presume competence. *Equity & Excellence in Education*, 39(2), 166–75.

Blume, H. (September 30, 1998). Neurodiversity: On the neurological underpinnings of geekdom. *The Atlantic*. Retrieved from www.theatlantic.com/magazine/ archive/1998/09/neuro diversity/5909.

CAST (n.d.). About Universal Design for Learning. Retrieved from http://www.cast
.org/our-work/about-udl.html#.XL3XyXdFzIV.

Charlton, J. (1998). *Nothing about us without us: disability, oppression and empowerment.* Berkeley: University of California Press.

Clare, E. (2017). *Brilliant imperfection: Grappling with cure.* Durham: Duke University Press.

Cohen, B. (2008). *Front of the class: How Tourette syndrome made me the teacher I
never had.* New York: St. Martin's Griffin.

Connor, D., and Bejoian, L. (2007). Crippling school curricular: 20 ways to re-teach
disability. *Review of Disability Studies*, 3(3), 3-13.

Couser, G. T. (2005). Disability, life narrative, and representation. *Publications of
Modern Language Associations*, 120(2), 602–6.

Crenshaw, K. (1989). *Demarginalizing the intersection of race and sex: A black feminist critique of antidiscrimination doctrine, feminist theory and antiracist politics.*
University of Chicago Legal Forum, 1(8). Available at: https://chicagounbound
.uchicago.edu/uclf/vol1989/iss1/8.

Daskal, L. (n.d.). *How a leader must challenge the status quo.* Retrieved from https://
www.lollydaskal.com/leadership/how-leader-must-challenge-the-status-quo/.

Davis, L. J. (September 25, 2011). Why is disability missing from the discourse on
diversity? Retrieved from https://www.chronicle.com/article/Why-Is-Disability
-Missing-From/129088.

Dudley-Marling, C. (2004). The social construction of learning disabilities. *Journal
of Learning Disabilities*, 37(6), 482–89.

Eddings Prince, D. (2010) An exceptional path: an ethnographic narrative reflecting on autistic parenthood from evolutionary, cultural, and spiritual perspectives.
Ethos, 38(1), 56-68.

Fadiman, A. (1997). *The spirit catches you and you fall down: A Hmong child, her
American doctors, and the collision of two cultures.* New York: Farrar, Straus and
Giroux.

Feshbach, N. D., and Feshbach, S, (2009). Empathy and education. In J. Decety and
W. Ickes (Eds.) *The social neuroscience of empathy*, pp. 85–98. Cambridge: The
MIT Press.

Groce, N. E. (1985). *Everyone here spoke sign language: Hereditary deafness on
Martha's vineyard.* Boston: Harvard University Press.

Haldane, H., and Crawford, D. (2010). What Lula lacks: Grappling with the discourse
of autism at home and in the field. *Anthropology Today*, 26(3), 24–26.

Hendrickx, S. (2010). *The adolescent and adult neuro-diversity handbook: Asperger's syndrome, ADHD, dyslexia, dyspraxia, and related conditions.* London:
Jessica Kingsley.

Higashida, N. (2016). *The reason I jump: The inner voice of a thirteen-year-old boy
with autism.* New York: Random House.

Ho, S. (2019, March 18). Canfei to canjo: The freedom of being loud. Retrieved from
https://www.bitchmedia.org/article/the-freedom-of-being-loud.

Kapp, S. (2011). Navajo and autism: the beauty of harmony. *Disability & Society*,
26(5), 583–95.

McIntosh, P. (July/August, 1989). White privilege: Unpacking the invisible knapsack. *Peace and Freedom Magazine,* 10–12.

Nieto, S. (2006). Solidarity, courage and heart: What teacher educators can learn from a new generation of teachers. *Intercultural Education,* 17(5), 457–73.

Oliver, N. (1990). *The politics of disablement.* New York: St. Martin's Press.

Pollak, D. (2009). *Neurodiversity in higher education: Positive responses to specific learning differences.* New York: Wiley.

Prince-Hughes, D. (2004). *Songs of the gorilla nation: My journey through autism.* New York: Three Rivers Press.

Rentenbach, B., Prislovsky, L., and Gabriel, R. (2017). Valuing differences: Neurodiversity in the classroom. *Phi Delta Kappan,* 98(8), 59–63.

Rioux, M., and Carbert, A. (2003). Human rights and disability: The international context. *Journal on Developmental Disabilities,* 10(2), 1–13.

Saks, E. (2008). *The center cannot hold: My journey through madness.* New York: Hachette Books.

Sanford, C., Newman, L., Wagner, M., Cameto, R., Knokey, A., Shaver, D., Buckely, J. A., and Yen, S. J. (2011). *The post-high school outcomes of young adults with disabilities up to 6 years after high school: Key findings from the national longitudinal transition study-2.* Washington, DC: National Center for Special Education Research.

Sapon-Shevin, M. (2003). Inclusion: A matter of social justice. *Educational Leadership,* 61, 25–28.

Singer, J. (1999). Why can't you be normal for once in your life?: From a problem with no name to a new category of difference, in M. Corker and S. French (Eds.), *Disability Discourse* (pp. 59–67). Buckingham: Open University Press.

Smith, E. (2006). The strength-based counseling model. *The Counseling Psychologist,* 34(1), 13–79.

Stone, J. (Ed.). (2005). *Culture and disability: Providing culturally competent services.* Thousand Oaks: Sage Publications.

Thornicroft, G., Brohan, E., Kassam, A., and Lewis-Holmes, E. (2008). Reducing stigma and discrimination: Candidate interventions. *International Journal of Mental Health Systems,* 2–3.

UPIAS. (1976). *Fundamental principles of disability.* London: Union of the Physically Impaired Against Segregation.

Valle, J. W., and Connor, D. J. (2011). *Rethinking disability: A disability studies approach to inclusive practices.* New York: McGraw-Hill.

Wolframe, P. M. (2013). The madwoman in the academy, or, revealing the invisible straightjacket: Theorizing and teaching saneism and sane privilege. *Disability Studies Quarterly,* 33(1), https://dsq-sds.org/article/view/3425/3200.

World Health Organization (2017). Retrieved from https://www.who.int/news-room/facts-in-pictures/detail/disabilities.

Chapter Two

Not Just Accommodating:
Pedagogy Beyond the Archetypical

Rory E. Kraft Jr. and Kevin Hermberg

Higher education is in the midst of making pedagogical changes to respond more fully to the needs of students through divergent learning methods and accommodating needs for students who have disabilities. Many incoming traditional-aged undergraduates may have had, since kindergarten, accommodations that reflect an understanding and appreciation of the nuances of divergent intellectual processing.

This is in contrast to the generally narrower range of accommodations in higher education. In the following chapter, the authors look at possible changes that individual faculty members can implement to provide an educational space where neurodiverse students can thrive. In doing so, it is helpful to consider three (anonymized) sketches of actual students encountered in the authors' classrooms to better understand the range of learning and cognitive styles captured by the diagnosis of being on the autism spectrum:

• Adam had not declared a major when he took Introduction to Philosophy. His written work was extremely well done; in class, he tended to be on the quiet side and refrained from making eye contact. After becoming a philosophy major, Adam surprised students in an ethics course when his oral presentation was dramatic, included long quotations from the text, and was done completely from memory. The only accommodation that Adam had registered with the college was for extra time on tests, though this was largely not an issue in the paper-driven philosophy courses he took for his major.
• Bruce appeared to be unconcerned by what others thought of him. He routinely wore capes on campus, ranging from well-made Victorian-style to less well-constructed ones that resembled hastily self-sewn garments.

He was never shy to participate in class, but his perspective and approach were often quite apart from the rest of the class. He excelled at thinking through theoretical complexities—such as the various categories of action in Aristotle's ethics—but was less well equipped to deal with spontaneous examples. While Bruce self-identified as having autism, he did not utilize any formal accommodations through the college's accessibility office.

- Charlotte was a student enrolled in a Logic course but was not a philosophy major. Such a course is often a struggle for students as it involves many of the types of reasoning that mathematics uses but, unlike with math, students have not had the benefit of years of practice in logic in their K-12 education. However, Charlotte was able to master the materials quite easily, which was noteworthy given that she never purchased the textbooks. She self-identified as having Asperger's syndrome and had a natural affinity for categories and deductions. She was not registered with the accessibility office and used no formal accommodations.

Adam, Bruce, and Charlotte would not likely have been encouraged to attend college a generation ago, but they are not atypical of a growing portion of the student population in higher education. Despite challenges presented by their autism spectrum disorder (ASD), such students have strengths that can benefit them educationally: strong memory, focus precision, dedication, analytic skills, remarkable powers of observation, sincerity/impartiality, and willingness to listen to others (Van Hees, Moyson, and Roeyers, 2015).

NEURODIVERSITY AND ASD

"Neurodiversity" is the label used to denote acceptance of those whose cognitive and perceptual processes differ from the "normal" (Silberman, 2015). Shearer (1981) developed this term to acknowledge the different modes of being for those on the autism spectrum, with dyslexia, with attention deficit hyperactive disorder (ADHD), with dyscalculia, and other conditions without holding their processes as deficient from the standard.

In a manner similar to the way the deaf community claimed a space for itself, those in the neurotribes differentiated themselves from the neurotypical without finding themselves as lacking or "less than." One can focus on those on the spectrum while remaining mindful of the problem of making generalized statements. The variety of ways in which neurodifferences can express themselves behaviorally leads to a common saying in the autism community: "If you've met one person with autism, you've met one person with autism."

ACCOMMODATIONS AND INCLUSIVITY

While much research has been done regarding the learning and educational experiences of children, the research into ASD in higher education is less voluminous. Van Hees, Moyson, and Roeyers (2015) studied the experiences of students with ASD in college or university settings. Based on that research, they make several institution-level recommendations:

- more extensive and effective coaching of students with ASD
- students should be involved in the transition planning to discuss which support has proved effective for them in the past and how that can be implemented in higher education
- individual coaching in the three domains of education, student life, and daily (independent) living, rather than training programs
- adequate individual psychological support to overcome mental health issues
- support groups where they can meet other students with ASD and where they can share experiences and discuss how they solve their problems.
- increased awareness among staff and students about ASD and the way in which it can affect navigating in college

These are good recommendations that ought to be pursued; however, they require significant institutional planning and resources and are, thus, both un-likely to happen quickly and outside the reach of many individual instructors.

Claxton, Claxton, Keith, and Yocum (2018) point to both the scope of the institutional resources that might be needed to accommodate such students and to the need for individual faculty to consider ways to augment institu-tional support. The absence or presence of academic accommodation and social support correlates with not only classroom success but also broader emotional markers of success.

Even when students successfully navigate the accommodations system in higher education, neurodiverse students often face "challenges that are not frequently addressed by the array of accommodations and tutoring services provided through the college" (Hart, Grigal, and Weir, 2010). As Barnhill (2016) points out, many colleges and universities "are not equipped to handle" the challenges faced by students on the autism spectrum, and "often the college disability offices are already stretched thin in resources and staff." This shifts the need for student support onto the faculty.

Christoff (2017) points to basic structures of philosophy courses that might be challenging to students who have received accommodations in other settings. From the heavily textual nature of philosophy to the need to quickly verbalize ideas in Socratic in-class discussions, philosophy has not traditionally been welcoming to those who have non-neurotypical cognitive processing or learning modalities.

Her consideration of approaches for an inclusive philosophy classroom is, in many ways, an engagement with the possibility of modifications to a set of courses and common pedagogical practices within a given discipline that might, when combined, lead to an environment that is welcoming to students with learning differences. If the techniques of educating students in philosophy can be modified to become more accepting of those with learning disabilities, it should be possible to do the same in other fields that are perhaps more welcoming.

A central difficulty faced in attempts to be inclusive in the neurodiversity sense is that the legal framework of reasonable accommodations is not well defined or understood. The majority of what college instructors are familiar with is extended time on exams, allowing exams to be written out of the classroom, and student use of recording devices or human aids in the classroom.

These sorts of accommodations do not help if the difficulty is moving from keeping and understanding information to using that information in a creative manner—from composing an essay giving one's own view to the "fun" project of depicting a concept visually. An additional difficulty could be discerning from nonverbal cues about which information in a classroom discussion is relevant and should be retained for future use.

Christoff focuses on "learning disabilities" while acknowledging that the term is perhaps overbroad. Among the aspects she groups into the term are those that point to the broader sense of neurodiversity—difficulty with reading, spelling, deduction, processing information quickly, expressing ideas in writing, and so on.

One of the subtler differences that Christoff points to is that the student with disabilities might not receive as much positive attention. This can vary from less feedback on writing to dismissive attitudes to classroom contributions. In some very real sense, it is these sorts of informal constraints on learning that will increase as a greater number of neurodiverse students move into college-level education.

Christoff provides recommendations for moving toward greater inclusivity. They are:

• Syllabus Statements—explicit communication that the instructor is open to adjustments other than those arranged by the Students with Disabilities Office and that reveals an instructor's sensitivity to the issues faced by ASD and intellectually disabled (ID) students. Christoff includes a six-point list of qualities/criteria for such statements.

- Presentation of Course Content—ensuring multiple methods of access and multiple means of presentation/representation, multiple means of engagement, multiple means of expression (she cites Rose and Meyer [2006] here).
- Classroom Technology—used to "aid instructors in implementing universal design." The discussion is about tech to stream videos, take clicker polls, project comics, and so forth. She engages a brief discussion here about the idea of banning phones and laptops in class but allowing them for students registered with Student Disability Services. (This last is potentially problematic by forcing students to choose between using an accommodation and being open to classmates about their need for such.)
- Learning Assessments—providing students "with multiple means of demonstrating their competency in the subject matter."
- Instructor/Student Relations—intentionally creating an empathetic relationship with students, including the disclosing of one's own disabilities and an acknowledgment that the instructor does not know the particulars of how a student's differences impact her learning.

It is important that instructors consider in each case that these recommendations are meant to provide more support of student learning, not simply move from one mode of learning to another and, perhaps, thereby disadvantaging a different set of students. Consider, for example, the call for alternative learning assessments. The key to Christoff's approach here is to provide options for students, not merely to move to a different (and perhaps equally problematic) assessment tool.

An instructor could, drawing on the work of Zemits (2017), develop a set of assessments that provided the opportunity for students to display their understanding of the concepts of a unit in a "creative" fashion. Some of these possibilities include creative mind maps of an argument/text or producing a mini-movie. The first might be well suited for a neurodiverse student to utilize in order to submit something instead of the usual essay or report. Depending on the specifics of one's placement on the spectrum, the second might well prove untenable.

College is sometimes understood to be the "last bridge before the real world," and as such, the problems of becoming more inclusive in the face of learning styles that are not common in the broader population is difficult (Farrell, 2004). How far this sort of coaching, mentoring, and acceptance should go is an open question. Perhaps by expanding upon Christoff's approach to an inclusive classroom, instructors can come to better approximate a learning space that allows for neurodiversity.

As instructors embrace neurodiversity and welcome divergent thinking and communication manners in the classroom, maybe we can come closer to a Freire-inspired classroom where the students and teachers learn from each other in true collaboration instead of through dominant power relations.

In contrast to what he terms "banking" systems of teaching that involve the transfer of knowledge from the expert to the novice, Freire (1970) advocated for an educational experience wherein all are learners and teachers. An example of how this can occur in the college classroom is the sort of close textual reading that frequently occurs in philosophy or literature classes. In the reading of the text, the place of expert is empty; all the members of the class (including the instructor) are reading together and discussing what the text means.

EXPANDING FROM CHRISTOFF

Key to an inclusive classroom that embraces neurodiversity is allowing for multiple methods of learning assessment. Of particular import for those on the spectrum are those assignments and assessments that minimize the need for displaying creative approaches that are extraneous to the outcome. Further, in-class discussions should be conducted in such a way that those who are not as comfortable confronting another are not penalized for nonparticipation.

Just as instructors ought to be mindful of those whose dyslexia (included in neurodiversity in the broadest sense) interferes with their ability to read new material aloud, they ought to be mindful of those whose approach to the world involves routine and rules. At the same time, instructors can embrace the possibilities that a neurodiverse classroom brings.

Those whose neuroprocessing leads to fascination with processes do well with assignments that focus on comparison of multiple drafts of a text (e.g., a comparison of the multiple drafts of Herman Melville's *Billy Budd*, noting the differences between the early and late versions of the unfinished work in a writing or literature course, or a comparison of the version of Mary Shelley's *Frankenstein* prior to Percy Shelly's involvement with the version that was originally published in a literature course or a course in gender studies).

One way to design assignments and projects that support every student in the class is to articulate the learning objectives and the specific content on which an assignment is based and have each student propose an assignment to meet those criteria. The details might look different in different disciplines, and the assignment posting might even offer some suggestions, including the prompt one would have written for a typical one-size-fits-all version of the assignment, after making it clear that students are encouraged to suggest alternatives of any conceivable sort.

While it is not possible in every context, one might have the students make their proposals in person by means of discussions in which they make the case that their assignment meets the learning objectives at hand. This discussion gives instructors the opportunity to begin to build the sort of individualized mentorship suggested by Van Hees, Moyson, and Roeyers (2015) and Christoff (2017). In other contexts, one might have the students submit a letter or video of support or justification along with assignment proposals.

This propose-your-own-assignment approach allows those who do better with modalities other than the traditional paper to suggest something else, and it does so without singling anyone out. Because the proposal includes students making the case that the project (be it an essay, video, painting, model, presentation to the class, or whatever else they conceive) meets the learning objectives, this procedure also has students reflecting on their learning and how they learn. This sort of metacognitive work is crucial to students becoming self-directed learners (Ambrose et al., 2010).

Depending on the course and the scale of the assignment (e.g., if it is the major assignment for the course), one could utilize a bit of class time, after students have gotten their particular approaches approved, having students conference with each other regarding what they are doing and why. This supports the point made by Scott, Mcguire, and Shaw (2003) that it is desirable in designing universally for students to interact and communicate with each other and their instructors.

CONCLUSION

Rather than think of inclusion as a sort of replacement for accommodation, instructors should find ways to see the skill sets and understandings that our students bring to the classroom and the course content to allow us all to come away with a sense that there are options befitting both the strengths and the challenges presented by neurodiversity. On a small scale, it might mean a professor re-reading Hume's *An Enquiry Concerning Human Understanding* with an awareness of how neurodiversity might challenge traditional understandings of epistemology.

On a larger scale, it might mean encouraging students to continue on with graduate-level work. Adam went on to earn a master's degree in philosophy. Not all students will fulfill the narrow range of what instructors see as their potential; being truly inclusive of differences involves accepting different life goals. Bruce left college without completing a degree and is happily working as a night stocker for a nationwide retail store. Charlotte was encouraged to consider advanced work in logic or mathematics and declined. She earned her degree and entered the business world.

REFERENCES

Ambrose, S., Bridges, M., DiPietro, M., Lovett, M., and Norman, M. (2010). *How learning works: Seven research-based principles for smart teaching.* San Francisco: Jossey-Bass.

Barnhill, G. (2016). Supporting students with Asperger syndrome on college campuses: Current practices. *Focus on Autism and Other Developmental Disabilities,* 31(1), 3–15.

Christoff, C. (2017). Beyond providing accommodations: How to be an effective instructor and ally to students with learning disabilities. *American Association of Philosophy Teachers Studies in Pedagogy,* 3, 8–32.

Claxton, B., Claxton, R., Keith, D., and Yocum, R. (2018). Support services for students with autism spectrum disorder in higher education. *Journal of College Orientation and Transition,* 25(1), 5–16.

Farrell, E. F. (2004). Asperger's confounds colleges. *Chronicle of Higher Education,* 51(7), A35–36.

Freire, P. (1970). *Pedagogy of the oppressed.* Trans. Myra Bergman Ramos. New York: Herder and Herder.

Hart, D., Grigal, M., and Weir, C. (2010). Expanding the paradigm: Postsecondary education options for individuals with autism spectrum disorder and intellectual disabilities. *Focus on Autism and Other Developmental Disabilities.* 25(3), 134–50.

Rose, D. H., and Meyer, A. (2006). *A practical reader in universal design for learning.* Cambridge: Harvard Education Press.

Scott, S. S., Mcguire, J. M., and Shaw, S. F. (2003). Universal design for instruction: A new paradigm for adult instruction in postsecondary education. *Remedial and Special Education,* 24(6), 369–79.

Shearer, A. (1981). *Disability, whose handicap?* London: Blackwell.

Silberman, S. (2015). *NeuroTribes: The legacy of autism and the future of neurodiversity.* New York: Avery.

Van Hees, V., Moyson, T., and Roeyers, H. (2015). Higher education experiences of students with autism spectrum disorder: Challenges, benefits and support needs. *Journal of Autism and Developmental Disorders,* 45, 1673–88.

Zemits, B. (2017). Representing knowledge: Assessment of creativity in Humanities. *Arts and Humanities in Higher Education,* 16(2), 173–87.

Part II

INCLUSION AND EXCLUSION

Chapter Three

Teaching Indigenous Sovereignty in Multicultural America

Danica Sterud Miller

Critical literacy and its interrogation of dominant ideologies as a major component of a university education in the last two decades are undisputed, and yet this same interrogation of dominant narratives often neglects American Indians and American Indian tribes within the contemporary landscape. If the goal of American diverse representation means striving toward a democratic ideal of equality, then conversely, for indigenous peoples, as colonized peoples living on colonized land, democratic equality is impossible.

Grande (2008) agrees: "Indigenous peoples have not, like other marginalized groups, been fighting for inclusion in the democratic imaginary, but, rather, for the right to remain distinct, sovereign, and tribal peoples" (p. 189). When American Indian texts are brought into the classroom, then those indigenous voices must be foregrounded by the contemporary state of colonization of indigenous peoples.[1]

This chapter examines how definitions of indigeneity and sovereignty are often contradictory to contemporary rhetoric of America as a melting pot of diversity and ends by proposing a few textual examples and lesson plans for integrating sovereignty into the higher education curriculum.

A little less than 10 percent of American Indians hold a bachelor's degree ("Reporters' Notebook: Native Americans Struggle," 2018). While there are many reasons for this abysmal percentage, educators in higher education cannot overlook their complicity in re-creating colonialism in academia. Gould (1992) rightly points out, "It is obvious that there is not a university in this country that is not built on what was once native land. We should reflect on this over and over, in order to understand this fact as one fundamental point about the relationship of Indians to academia" (p. 81–82).

Without consciously acknowledging our colonial past and colonial present in our classrooms, indigenous erasure continues. Academia profits from the land theft and genocide of American Indians. By creating classrooms that acknowledge colonialism and work toward an understanding of American Indian sovereignty, academia helps to decolonize power structures and build space where American Indian students are welcomed. This is a small gesture toward the debt that academia owes Indigenous America, and it is just one of the many steps higher education needs to take to facilitate American Indian student retention.

What is indigeneity, and what does it mean to be indigenous in the twenty-first century? While there are many tribally specific ways to define an indigenous person, for the purposes of this work, indigenous peoples have a land-based epistemology traumatized by settler colonialism. Land cannot be understood as separate from indigeneity.

According to Deloria and Lytle (1998), "It is important to understand the primacy of land in the Indian psychological makeup, because, as land is alienated, all other forms of social cohesion also begin to erode, land having been the context in which the other forms have been created" (p. 12). However, because of the brutal history of settler colonialism—genocide, boarding schools, forced removal from ancestral homelands, and so on—many indigenous peoples have been cut off from their indigenous communities and epistemologies.

American Indians are generally included in most discussions on diversity and ethnicity, but for many American Indians, certainly most American Indians with personally recognized and acknowledged tribal community affiliations, American Indians are not only part of an ethnic group within the larger United States, but instead, they are members of nations in an active state of settler colonization continually committed by the now United States.

Barker (2005) states: "The racialization of the Indian is the erasure of our sovereignty," and it is important for any teachings that include American Indians to understand that the construct of an American Indian race (as opposed to Indigenous nations) is the direct result of colonial efforts to reduce American Indian tribal landholdings (p. 17). Indeed, Indigenous nations continued and continue to construct themselves as sovereign peoples.

Deloria and Lytle (1998) argue that the primary term behind sovereignty, nationhood, "implies a process of decision making that is free and uninhibited within the community, a community in fact that is almost completely insulated from external factors as it considers its possible options" (p. 13–14), which Indigenous communities have continued to do even in the face of constant trauma from settler colonialism.

Among many reasons, but the creation of a false blood distinction as an inherent indicator of Indianness most importantly, the ahistorization of American Indians outside of a rhetoric of sovereignty and indigeneity into a racialized ethnicity became absolutely a process of colonization (and, thus, land theft and genocide). It is crucial that when teaching about American Indian tribal communities in the classroom that American Indian tribal communities are historicized within their indigenous sovereignties or teachers will only contribute to the continuation of indigenous colonization.

INDIGENOUS SOVEREIGNTY AND
RHETORIC OF DIVERSITY

When the inherent link between indigeneity and sovereignty is misunderstood or unexplained, indigeneity itself is rendered moot. King (2012) points out that, "At the core, teaching with rhetorical sovereignty and rhetorical alliance asks us to do the difficult and challenging work of calling institutionalized racism as we see it, even in our own work, and undoing the erasure that multiculturalism tends to wreak on Native writers and Native texts" (p. 230).

Keeping this in mind, the goal of including American Indian texts in the higher education multicultural classroom becomes less about a democratic ideal and more of a project of inclusivity. To teach inclusivity then is to understand that even as American Indians are a part of American history, indigeneity, simultaneously, if seemingly contradictorily, means to be a part of the now United States and, yet, to be separate and unique.

Using both of these historical premises, the Proclamation of Alcatraz (1969) addresses these histories while also leading students toward a contemporary understanding of American Indians through the Indigenous act of "rhetorical sovereignty."[2] Lyons (2000) defines rhetorical sovereignty as "the inherent right of [indigenous] peoples to determine their own communicative needs and desires" (p. 449). This "inherent right"—that is, indigenous sovereignty—is expressed through various rhetoric.

When analyzing the textual production of American Indians and their communities, it behooves educators to look for rhetorics of sovereignty and ask how these texts express indigenous sovereignty.

RHETORICAL SOVEREIGNTY LESSON PLAN

While the following lesson works well using only the Proclamation of Alcatraz, if time and inclination permits, a reading of most any United States treaty with an Indigenous nation will work, though using the treaty the host university resides upon helps facilitate for students the sense of indigeneity and what indigenous nations have lost through treaty abuses and genocidal policies.

Even if time doesn't permit, leading with the following questions will help facilitate understanding of the Proclamation. Helpful questions: What key language and words are used? What are the rhetorical strategies used in a treaty? Why do nations write treaties?[3] What does a treaty accomplish at the time of the signing versus what does a treaty accomplish hundreds of years later?

If students are consistently analyzing the treaty from a settler-colonial perspective, ask them to respond to the following quote by Russell (2008): "American Indians became literal prisoners of treaty discourse. Moreover, Indian reservations became the loci of imprisoned peoples who could be guarded rather easily and, if necessary, annihilated" (p. 3).

After an introduction to treaties and treaty language, briefly introduce students to the Occupation of Alcatraz, an almost two-year indigenous occupation of unused and unwanted federal land. The Indians of All Tribes claimed the inhospitable old prison by citing the Treaty of Fort Laramie (1868), which promised to return to the Sioux all former Sioux land that had been retired and abandoned by the federal government.

When the Alcatraz Federal Penitentiary closed in 1963, the United States declared the island surplus federal property, which, in turn, the Indians of All Tribes declared to be Indian land. While the legal backing the Indians of All Tribes cited was rather flimsy, the motivation was not.

After this discussion, have students read the Proclamation of Alcatraz. Here are a few useful guiding questions to facilitate an understanding of the Proclamation of Alcatraz as a production of textual rhetorical sovereignty: What do students notice about the language in the Proclamation? How does it both reflect and undermine the rhetorics used by treaty writers of previous centuries? And what does this imply about the writers of the Proclamation? What are their histories? And how are they enacting rhetorical sovereignty?

It is important to notice that this was written by the Indians of All Tribes, which purposely evokes both the attempt by settler colonialism to racialize Indigenous peoples and shows that through such an attempt to erase multiple indigenous histories, a type of resistance through unity across indigenous communities can be found.

After these questions are probed and prodded, it helps to return to one of the earlier questions: What does a treaty accomplish at the time of the signing versus what does a treaty accomplish hundreds of years later? If, as Russell suggests, Indians are prisoners of treaties, how does "rhetorical sovereignty" decolonize treaty discourse? Students should understand that by using treaty discourse, the Proclamation of Alcatraz decolonizes treaty discourse by invoking treaty language in order to legitimize the Occupation, much as treaties themselves legitimized (and continue to legitimize) the outright theft of American Indian land.

Russell (2008) further notes that, "In a type of cosmic irony, those same treaties meant to usurp and disinherit Indians of their ancestral lands resources were interpreted in the twentieth century to promote Indian sovereignty. The treaties' language hadn't changed one iota, but how they were read changed completely" (p. 2). Many of the occupiers of Alcatraz were students and academics and tribal leaders. The occupiers were well-read and knew their treaties, and certainly, they knew their treaties much better than the settlers currently occupying indigenous land.

The imagery and references of the Proclamation of Alcatraz immediately remind the reader of this fact. The occupiers understand their rights as sovereign peoples both as a construction of their ancestral rights and as a construction of Western federal treaties. This might be an appropriate time to remind students that the United States has broken all of the over five hundred treaties it has made with indigenous nations. From an indigenous lens, how does treaty-breaking affect the relationship and trust between the sovereign entities? And how might that anger and resentment fuel such acts as takeovers and occupations?

The next goal of the lesson is to analyze the lens of the Indians of All Tribes. In what ways are they constructing their sovereignty? A helpful addition to the Proclamation of Alcatraz is to include the letter that accompanied the Proclamation when the Indians of All Tribes sent it to various news outlets and governmental agencies. While the Proclamation itself is a rather satirical take on treaties, the accompanying letter suggests a different type of rhetorical sovereignty.

The letter begins by stating the reason for the Occupation: "We moved onto Alcatraz Island because we feel that Indian people need a Cultural Center of their own. For several decades, Indian people have not had enough control of training their young people. And without a cultural center of their own, we are afraid that the old Indian ways may be lost. We believe that the only way to keep them alive is for Indian people to do it themselves." How is the tone different here from the Proclamation? What are the Indians of All Tribes accomplishing here that is different from the Proclamation?

While the Proclamation engages in a type of rhetorical sovereignty by acknowledging the ancestral sovereignty discussed in the treaties, the letter takes it one step further by now participating in a rhetorical sovereignty that takes possession of the present and future. Sovereignty is a construction and a continual process. As King (2015) reminds us: "Every new site, new context, new speaker, and new goal will require a shift in what sovereignty means, remaining rooted in its histories but also looking forward to preserve the integrity of indigenous nations and communities" (p. 21).

Importantly, the Indians of All Tribes invoke this seeming dichotomy at the beginning of their letter: "So we must start somewhere. We feel that if we are going to succeed, we must hold on to the old ways. *This is the first and most important reason we went to Alcatraz Island.*" The Indians of All Tribes are constructing a sovereign future by referencing the sovereign past. Deloria and Lytle (1998) discuss the distinction between United States communities and indigenous communities: "As nation-peoples, the priority was not primarily individual rights but the survival and continuity of the community, its culture, and its land" (p. 20).

It is through ancestral sovereignty that the Indians of All Tribes enact rhetorical sovereignty for the now and future: "We feel that the only reason Indian people have been able to hold on and survive through decades of persecution and cultural deprivation is that the Indian way of life is and has been strong enough to hold the people together."

For further discussion, how does the Indian of All Tribes suggest a sovereign future? What practical and theoretical answers do they propose? The Indians of All Tribes are working together as one people not because of the federal racialization of Indians to decrease landholdings but with the intention of increasing resistance and power: "We are issuing this call in an attempt to unify all our Indian Brothers behind a common cause." This is not a racializing of indigenous peoples; it is an alliance across indigenous nations: "We realize too that we are not getting anywhere fast by working alone as individual tribes.

"If we can gather together as brothers and come to a common agreement, we feel that we can be much more effective, doing things for ourselves." What are the differences, students should be asked, between the federal racialization of Indians and a common Indian cause, as expressed by the letter? What are sovereign gains in such an alliance? And perhaps, what could hurt indigenous communities through such alliances?

CONCLUSION

Using these brief histories of indigenous peoples and their relationship with the United States works well as a primer for introducing American Indian texts in the higher education classroom.

A lens of indigeneity avoids repeating the erasure of American Indian sovereignty, and also, by using an indigenous lens, the higher education classroom becomes less alienating and more welcoming to American Indian students. Grande (2008) points out that:

> the deep structures of the "pedagogy of oppression" fail to consider American Indians as [a] categorically different population, virtually incomparable to other minority groups. [This is] to call attention to the fundamental difference of what it means to be a sovereign and tribal people within the geopolitical confines of the United States (p. 183).

The more the higher education classroom becomes inclusive, the more important it becomes to understand that inclusivity includes peoples, especially indigenous peoples, who may or may not want to be included. Why they are hesitant, and what are their separate but concurrent histories, must always be addressed.

NOTES

1. This chapter uses American Indian to describe the Indigenous peoples of the now United States in order to foreground the contemporary and active state of colonial state of Indigenous peoples and rejects the usage of Native American because Native American implies democratic American identity.

2. Full text of the Proclamation of Alcatraz and the Letter available at http://www.historyisaweapon.com/defcon1/alcatrazproclamationandletter.html.

3. If time and student interest allow, have students analyze the following quote that addresses the importance of nation-building through treaty-making by Vine Deloria, Jr.: "The American Revolution revived the idea of Indian sovereignty. Although reciting polite phrases about the equality of man, the American revolutionaries were plainly outside the law of civilized societies in their revolt, and to gain respectability they adopted the most acceptable posture [treaties] to Indians possible with the hope that by demonstrating their ability to act in traditional political terms they could allay the fears of other nations so as to legitimize their activities" ("Self Determination and the Concept of Sovereignty," in *Economic Development on Indian Reservations*).

REFERENCES

Barker, J. (2005). For whom sovereignty matters. In J. Barker (Ed), *Sovereignty matters: Locations of contestation and possibility in indigenous struggles for self-determination* (pp. 1–31). Lincoln: University of Nebraska Press.

Deloria, V., Jr. (1979). Self-determination and the concept of sovereignty. In R. D. Ortiz (Ed), *Economic development in American Indian reservations* (pp. 22–28). Albuquerque: University of New Mexico Press.

Deloria, V., Jr., and Lytle, C. (1998). *The nations within: The past and future of American Indian sovereignty.* Austin: University of Texas Press.

Gould, J. (1992). The problem of being "Indian": One mixed-blood's dilemma. In S. Smith and J. Watson (Eds.), *De/colonizing the subject: The politics of gender in women's autobiography* (pp. 81–90). Minneapolis: University of Minnesota Press.

Grande, S. (2008). Red pedagogy. In N. Denzin, Y. Lincoln, and L. Smith (Eds.), *Handbook of critical & Indigenous methodologies* (pp. 233–254). Thousand Oaks, CA: SAGE.

King, L. (2012). Rhetorical sovereignty and rhetorical alliance in the writing classroom: Using American Indian texts. *Pedagogy, 12* (2), 209–233. Durham: Duke University Press.

King, L. (2015). Keywords for teaching indigenous texts. In L. King, R. Gublee, and J. R. Anderson (Eds), *Survivance, sovereignty, and story: Teaching American Indian rhetorics* (pp. 17–34). Boulder, CO: Utah State University Press.

Lyons, S. R. (2000). Rhetorical sovereignty: What do American Indians want from writing? *College Composition and Communication, 51* (3), 447–68.

Proclamation of Alcatraz and Letter. (1969). Retrieved from http://www.history-isaweapon.com/defcon1/alcatrazproclamationandletter.html

Reporters' notebook: Native Americans struggle, build pride. (2018). Retrieved from https://www.educationworld.com/a_issues/schools/schools012.shtml

Russell, C. (2008). The paradox of sovereignty: Contingencies of meaning in American Indian treaty discourse. *American Indian Culture and Research Journal, 32* (1), 1–19.

Chapter Four

The Paradox of Inclusion and Exclusion

Samira Garcia, Tabitha McCoy, and Hoa Nguyen

While the concept of diversity has received increasing attention over the last fifty years (Hackett and Hogg, 2014), equity and inclusion are now entering the dialogue on human relationships. "Diversity" is often defined based on markers of difference and sameness that exist within and between groups. "Equity" is the fair and just treatment of all people in institutional processes, procedures, and distribution of resources (D5 Coalition, 2014). Practices and policies that remove the barriers that prevent the participation of all individuals promote equity.

"Inclusion" is the process of cultivating an environment in which diverse groups are fully able to participate and contribute (Ferdman, 2017). Thus, while an inclusive society necessitates diversity, a diverse society may not be inclusive or just.

In this chapter, the authors introduce the paradox of inclusion/exclusion to frame a discussion regarding the challenges they face when infusing equity, diversity, and inclusion (EDI) in the classroom. Techniques used to address these challenges are also introduced. Educators dedicated to embodying the principles of equity and inclusion are familiar with the process of deciding which issues and theories will be included/excluded in their curriculum—this is the paradox of inclusion/exclusion.

When making distinctions between sanctioned/unsanctioned values, educators might be teaching exclusion rather than inclusion (Stewart, Crary, and Humberd, 2008). Educators often experience the tension within this paradox.

CHALLENGES IN FACILITATING
EDI IN THE CLASSROOM

Designing a course curriculum that exemplifies EDI can include certain challenges. Below is a summary of some challenges experienced by the authors, which might be relevant to readers across many fields.

Encountering Requests for Exclusionary Dominant Discourse

Educators may encounter students who request that perspectives representative of privileged dominant discourses be included in the course content. Often, these are exclusionary ideas and frames of reference. The educator must evaluate the significance of including them in the curriculum and decide whether to honor the student's request.

While many consider the inclusion of dominant discourse a part of EDI, educators must consider that the act of this request is itself a privileged position, perpetuating a status quo outside of the classroom. Students with controversial ideas that do not fit the current political status quo may be less likely to make these requests (Garber, 1995).

For instance, consider the rise in phone calls to police reporting African Americans as potential criminals in the United States. Many of these calls are unfounded. However, this trend has become increasingly visible in the current US political climate, where policy is geared toward questioning ethnic minorities' privileges and rights. The calls are tolerated within a culture of white privilege that insufficiently challenges a harmful, false discourse about African Americans. In this instance, this should be exposed for what it is and not tolerated.

Similarly, in the classroom, educators should be mindful of assertions that masquerade as "normal" but are actually attempts to pull the classroom discussion back to a harmful stereotype that may also be a cultural norm. When considering student requests, educators should acknowledge the student's social location and the effect that honoring such requests may have on classroom culture.

Honoring "Free Speech" to Promote Student Engagement

Educators may still feel inclined to honor such requests for fear of violating students' right to free speech. Or they may be influenced by outside sources, such as institutional factors, promotion and tenure guidelines, student retention, and campus culture. The administrative bodies under which educators perform their duties might not provide appropriate training and opportunities to engage in EDI conversations, leaving educators ill-equipped to handle such requests (Sue, Torino, Capodilupo, Rivera, and Lin, 2009).

When educators adopt a "free speech at-all-cost" philosophy, it becomes increasingly difficult to be culturally responsive. There is only one response option available—to accept all utterances and discourses without consideration for sociocultural factors, power and privilege dynamics, and systematic marginalization.

Further, engagement in the classroom does not necessarily lead to or is representative of inclusion and integration (Hurtado, Ruiz Alvarado, and Guillermo-Wann, 2015). Therefore, indiscriminately allowing all utterances for the sake of student engagement may promote segregation rather than inclusiveness.

Encountering Narrow Definitions of EDI

The aforementioned challenges focus on circumstantial variables. However, the authors posit that each of the previous two challenges is indicative of narrow definitions of EDI. Narrow definitions inform what can and cannot be done and by whom. One student may feel able to request the inclusion of privileged, dominant discourses, while another may not.

Educators may experience difficulties in determining what should and should not be challenged. The educator's personal characteristics and sense of self can influence such decisions. Furthermore, educators who are part of a minority group may be socially trained to honor privileged requests. Conversely, educators who belong to a non-minority group may doubt their ability to facilitate EDI conversations (Sue, Torino, Capodilupo, Rivera, and Lin, 2009). The narrow definition here is that only those in minority positions, with firsthand experience of marginalization, can legitimately facilitate effective EDI conversations.

TEACHING EDI

Much like other group settings, interactions that take place within the classroom are informed by the larger social contexts. Within those contexts, each member, including the educator, brings with them their own epistemology. Interactions are shaped by the inequalities of power, equity, and diversity among members. As educators, how do we decide what to include or exclude in our conversations about equity and diversity?

When educators make a conscious decision to include particular ideas, they are simultaneously choosing to exclude others and vice versa. Due to its paradoxical nature, teaching EDI requires educators to become creative in their efforts to interrupt the normal hierarchies found within larger social contexts (Cannon, 1990).

Scholars have addressed the numerous ways educators may become creative in their efforts to teach EDI, the potential challenges of teaching EDI, as well as the inherent role of the educator in shaping conversations and learning of EDI. There have been discussions about the use of social constructionism as a framework in the classroom when addressing EDI. McDowell and Shelton (2002) note that discussions regarding social constructionism allow educators to engage their students in meaningful conversations that explore dominant social discourses.

In similar efforts to deconstruct habitual ways of thinking and learning within the classroom, some scholars address the need to pay careful attention to the global and local issues of EDI (Hernandez-Wolfe, Acevedo, Victoria, and Volkmann, 2015) and suggest opening space for a collaborative learning experience as a way to cultivate cultural equity, humility, reflexivity, and responsiveness.

Scholars have also addressed barriers to teaching EDI, such as white fragility (DiAngelo, 2011; Masko and Bloem, 2017) and white fatigue (Flynn, 2015). Educators of EDI play an important role in shaping the classroom learning environment (Beitin, Duckett, and Fackina, 2008) and have the opportunity to set the stage for meaningful dialogue. Since educators are facilitating conversations regarding various sensitive EDI issues, preparation is crucial when teaching EDI (Valerio, 2001).

Beitin and colleagues (2008) suggest professors discuss their own barriers to teaching, learning, and discussing issues surrounding EDI. Situated in a position of power, educators have the opportunity to share with students their struggles, mistakes, and how they have come to know what they know.

An Illustration of the Inclusion/Exclusion Paradox

In navigating the process of the paradox of inclusion and exclusion, the authors are reminded of a team-building exercise that illustrates the process (see Figure 1). In the exercise, participants are instructed to transport a large plastic bucket with the use of bungee cords. The facilitator positions participants around a bucket and bungee cords and instructs them to collectively move the bucket from one point to another.

With the use of the cords, the participants create the necessary tension to grasp, lift, and move the bucket. While too much tension tightens the grip and flips the bucket, too little tension loosens the participants' grip of the bucket. It is the relationship between the tightening and loosening of tension that

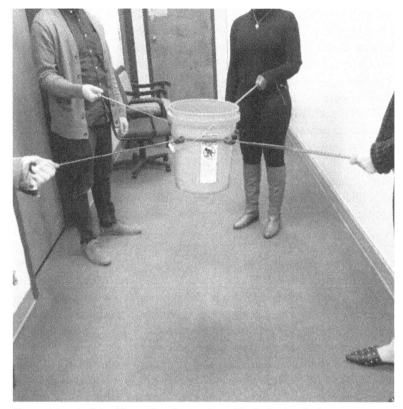

Figure 4.1. Activity illustrating the tension of inclusion/exclusion.

provides movement to complete the task. Participants must also respond to each other's actions to maintain the appropriate amount of tension.

Educators can use this as an experiential activity to illustrate the process of inclusion/exclusion in the classroom. The paradox lies in the symbiotic connection between inclusion and exclusion, such that one cannot exist without the other (M. Laughlin, personal communication, February 22, 2016). Inclusion is not possible without the critical examination and imperative renunciation of exclusionary ideas that threaten a culture of EDI. Within this paradox, there is an inevitable tension through which we can begin to make sense of exclusion as a crucial component in EDI classrooms.

Addressing Challenges by Embracing Tensions

The truth is that there is no easy, singular fix for the challenges educators face when facilitating EDI conversations. The authors suggest that educators embrace tensions created by these challenges by adopting a position informed by transparency and collaboration. This position requires that educators bring challenges to the forefront of class conversations, involving and engaging students in a critical examination of the process (rather than simply the content) of EDI conversations.

What follows are four ideas about how this may be done: first, naming the inclusion/exclusion paradox; second, fostering conscious awareness of sociopolitical context; third, focusing on classroom culture, rather than specific interactions; and fourth, including people while excluding oppressive dialogue.

First, educators should name, for themselves, the inclusion/exclusion paradox and how it informs pedagogy and teaching practices before setting foot in the classroom. Acknowledging the paradox throughout course planning, preparation, and implementation aids educators in the construction of a comprehensive, cohesive EDI classroom. Course curricula should include transparency in order to flatten unhelpful hierarchical structures between educators and students.

Consideration for student feedback and procedures for collecting feedback should be built into the course organization as well. Educators should remain open and respond to student contributions while being aware that not all contributions are helpful or should be implemented.

Educators should also anticipate and account for their own struggles in facilitating the EDI classroom. One way to do this is by intentionally engaging in processing conversations pre- and post-lectures with colleagues. In this way, educators can open up space for their own "thinking through" of EDI materials, topics, and processes.

Students also benefit from acknowledging the paradox of inclusion/ exclusion and the tension that resides in it. In being transparent about his or her own experience with this paradox, the educator models and opens reflective space for students to do the same. Practicing transparency demystifies the educator's processes, allowing for effective delivery of materials for students (Black, Wygonik, and Frey, 2011). Letting students know that EDI conversations can be challenging yet equally beneficial for the educator allows for a more collaborative "in-it-together" classroom culture.

This approach marks the difference between the educator inviting students into EDI conversation (which allows power to reside solely with the educator) and *entering into* EDI conversations with students, a more collaborative and inclusive approach (Polanco, personal communication, June 23, 2018).

Second, while aiming for inclusive dialogue, educators are still accountable for fostering and encouraging a safe environment. Accounting for sociopolitical contexts of historical privilege and oppression is necessary to meet this goal. Educators should be cognizant of the political platform most exclusionary views have been built upon.

Calling attention to the societal processes that construct and maintain these views while challenging the narrowness of the space they provide for alternative views is vital for the EDI classroom. If educators fail to account for the sociopolitical context of exclusionary views, they are at risk of sabotaging their efforts toward EDI.

The authors believe that it is important to avoid re-creating the unbalanced representation of ideas that leads to further marginalizing alternative truths and experiences. This means that educators must actively engage their critical judgment skills in deciding what should be included in the classroom. Students will have a variety of identities from cohort to cohort, for this is an ongoing process. What works one semester may not work the next.

The authors conceptualize this process as a flexible—ebb and flow—of changing dynamics as our sociopolitical context constricts and expands certain views throughout the years. In practice, maintaining awareness of current events and social trends such as hashtag movements (e.g., #MeToo and Black Lives Matter) can help educators foster this consciousness.

Three, researchers indicate that accounting for equality/inclusion while constructing classroom norms and employing cultural pluralism is beneficial for positive outcomes in multicultural classrooms (Schwarzenthal, Schachner, van de Vijver, and Juang, 2018). As educators and supervisors, the authors agree. Specific interactions with particular students, such as sidebar conversations, can help soothe student-educator anxiety and repair any ruptures in the teaching relationship.

However, the authors believe that this is insufficient. Building a classroom culture of collaboration and safe exploration may reduce the probability of such ruptures happening in the first place. Or, when they do occur, repair can happen in the classroom involving the whole community of stakeholders (educator and students).

Cultural pluralism allows for a both/and approach to the diversity of ideas and identities in the classroom. Seemingly contradictory ideas are allowed to exist together in one space, with each being examined critically and in context. The authors believe that fostering cultural pluralism can flatten the hierarchical categorization of identities. To do so, educators must be intentional about how time is distributed in the classroom.

This means that in certain situations, student participation must be appropriately limited. In other situations, it should be greatly encouraged. Yet, in most instances, the educator and students will be able to monitor and balance the narratives in the classroom through predetermined rules that include respect, gentle challenging, and relational understanding. This last point speaks to the authors' final suggestion. Educators must distinguish between including a person (as a sentient being) while simultaneously excluding oppressive dialogue.

Finally, educators need to think about including people and excluding oppressive dialogue. This last point is probably the hardest of the four suggestions. It is impossible to separate a person from their ideas and identity, as it is their worldview that makes them known to those with whom they are in a relationship. Nevertheless, it is important for both educators and classmates to realize that worldviews can evolve, given sufficient space for reflection.

This means that as each participating person in the classroom brings forth their ideas and notions, those listening should remain genuinely curious about how these make sense given the speaker's context. The absence of curiosity leads to opposition and defensiveness. It also leads to the totalizing of identities based on specific utterances.

It is the listener's responsibility to be positioned as a curious inquisitor of what is being said, who is saying it, what is being heard, and who is hearing it. This positioning is facilitated by the willingness to ask what is activating curiosity, opposition, or any other response in oneself as a listener. Understanding of one's own context may facilitate an understanding of the speaker's context as well. This humanizing position can then lead to open exploration rather than defensiveness and invalidation of the other.

CONCLUSION

As educators and students hold more empathetic and humanizing positions, they can engage more fully with each other in EDI dialogues. This holistic view redistributes the power between the listener(s) and speaker(s) and encourages a togetherness in cultivating a shared conversational space. In the process, listeners and speakers embody the paradox, both intrapersonally (tensions within themselves) and interpersonally (tensions between each other).

Rather than seeing oppositional views as polarization, students and educators can recognize these tensions as necessary diversity dynamics in EDI classrooms. By embracing the paradoxical nature of inclusion/exclusion, educators and students can understand and "accept the intimate connection between the two sides" (Ferdman, 2017, p. 248).

REFERENCES

Beitin, B., Duckett, R., and Fackina, P. (2008). Discussions of diversity in a class-room: A phenomenological study of students in an MFT training program. *Contemporary Family Therapy*, 30(4), 251–68. doi:10.1007/s10591-008-9072-4.

Black, L. J., Wygonik, M. L., and Frey, B. A. (2011). Faculty-preferred strategies to promote a positive classroom environment. *Journal of Excellence in College Teaching*, 22(2), 1–26.

Cannon, L. W. (1990). Fostering positive race, class, and gender dynamics in the classroom. *Women's Studies Quarterly*, 18(1/2), 126–34.

D5 Coalition. (2014). What is DEI? Retrieved from http://www.d5coalition.org/tools/dei/.

DiAngelo, R. (2011). White fragility. *The International Journal of Critical Pedagogy*, 3(3), 54–70.

Ferdman, B. M. (2017). Paradoxes of inclusion: Understanding and managing the tensions of diversity and multiculturalism. *The Journal of Applied Behavioral Science*, 53(2), 235–63. doi:10.1177/0021886317702608.

Flynn Jr., J. E. (2015). White fatigue: Naming the challenge in moving from an individual to a systemic understanding of racism. *Multicultural Perspectives*, 17(3), 115–24. doi:10.1080/15210960.2015.1048341.

Garber, M. A. (1995). Old wine in new bottles: The constitutional status of unconstitutional speech. *Vanderbilt Law Review*, 48, 349–87.

Hackett, J. D., and Hogg, M. A. (2014). The diversity paradox: When people who value diversity surround themselves with like-minded others. *Journal of Applied Social Psychology*, 44(6), 415–22. doi:10.1111/jasp.12233.

Hernandez-Wolfe, P., Acevedo, V. E., Victoria, I., and Volkmann, T. (2015). Transnational family therapy training: A collaborative learning experience in cultural equity and humility. *Journal of Feminist Family Therapy*, 27(3–4), 134–55. doi:10.1080/08952833.2015.1092813.

Hurtado, S., Ruiz Alvarado, A., and Guillermo-Wann, C. (2015). Creating inclusive environments: The mediating effect of faculty and staff validation on the relationship of discrimination/bias to students' sense of belonging. *Journal Committed to Social Change on Race and Ethnicity*, 1(1), 60–80.

Masko, A. L., and Bloem, P. L. (2017). Teaching for equity in the milieu of white fragility: Can children's literature build empathy and break down resistance? *Curriculum and Teaching Dialogue*, 19(1/2), 55–171.

McDowell, T., and Shelton, D. (2002). Valuing ideas of social justice in MFT curricula. *Contemporary Family Therapy*, 24(2), 313–31. doi:10.1023/A:1015351408957.

Schwarzenthal, M., Schachner, M. K., van de Vijver, F., and Juang, L. P. (2018). Equal but different: Effects of equality/inclusion and cultural pluralism on intergroup outcomes in multiethnic classrooms. *Cultural Diversity and Ethnic Minority Psychology*, 24(2), 260–71. doi:10.1037/cdp0000173.

Stewart, M. M., Crary, M., and Humberd, B. K. (2008). Teaching value in diversity: On the folly of espousing inclusion, while practicing exclusion. *Academy of Management Learning & Education*, 7(3), 374–86. doi:10.5465/amle.2008 .34251674.

Sue, D. W., Torino, G. C., Capodilupo, C. M, Rivera, D. P., and Lin, A. I. (2009). How white faculty perceive and react to difficult dialogues on race: Implications for teaching and training. *The Counseling Psychologist*, 37(8), 1090–115. doi:10.1177/ 001000009340443.

Valerio, N. L. (2001). Creating safety to address controversial issues: Strategies for the classroom. *Multicultural Education*, 8(3), 24–28.

Part III

TECHNOLOGY AND SOCIAL ACTION

Chapter Five

From Awareness to Action: Creating PSAs to Promote EDI

Stephanie L. Burrell Storms, Jay Rozgonyi,
and Kathi Rainville

In *Breaking Down Silos*, the authors describe common learning objectives for education promoting equity, diversity, and inclusion (EDI) (Hartwell et al., 2017). These objectives are increasing students' awareness, knowledge, and skills about issues of equity and justice on individual and institutional levels in society. The fourth objective—social action engagement—focuses on moving students from awareness about EDI to responding to various forms of social injustice (e.g., racism, sexism, heterosexism, etc.) (Burrell Storms, 2014).

Social action engagement (1) can be self-directed (e.g., confronting one's own bias), (2) focused on others (e.g., educating others about EDI), and/or (3) with an organization, for example, work to end homelessness (Alimo, 2012).

Helping students move along the continuum from awareness to action is a challenge in the EDI classroom for several reasons. First, EDI concepts might be new for students and seen as too abstract to understand. Other students might resist the topic due to their positionality (i.e., predominantly privileged identities) in the cycle of oppression. Moreover, issues about EDI may be absent from students' academic programs, making them seem unimportant or nonexistent. However, recent studies show students enrolled in social justice education courses show more confidence (Alimo, 2012) and commitment toward social action (Gurin-Sands, Gurin, Nagda, and Osuna, 2012).

In this chapter, the authors describe how a collaboration across two disciplines—social justice education (SJE) and educational technology (EDT)—led to a new assignment that engaged students enrolled in the SJE course in a social action project—creating public service announcements (PSAs) to promote EDI. While this chapter describes the project from the perspective of the SJE course in which it was taught, the authors point to its broader applicability across disciplines.

PROVIDING SOME CONTEXT

Promoting social justice is part of the mission at the Jesuit institution where this collaboration takes place. Through service and academic activities, students are expected to become socially aware citizens who work in solidarity with under-resourced communities to build equity across multiple institutions.

Furthermore, the graduate school of education, where the courses are housed, stresses the following tenets as key to training professional educators: (1) *belief in the inherent worth and dignity of each person; (2) commitment to greater good through service; and (3) advocacy as change agents and/or leaders within the chosen profession.* The goals of the PSA assignment reflect the mission of the school and university and might be similar to other institutional missions with social justice goals.

The authors are in the same educator preparation department. However, one teaches in the educational technology program, and the other teaches foundational courses. The authors imagine, depending on a professor's level of comfort with technology, the PSA could be assigned in a course taught by one professor (as in this case), or by professors from different disciplines where one could bring in the EDI content and the other with technological expertise.

ANSWERING THE CALL

In the summer of 2016, the educational technology instructor designed a new special topics course titled "Creating and Curating Digital Course Materials." One of the primary course outcomes was for students to "learn to operate as a technical expert in the role of course designer, under the direction of a faculty member who will function as the instructor and content expert." The instructor believed it was necessary for students enrolled in the course to experience how they would collaborate with teachers across subject areas in schools developing curricular projects.

Therefore, he invited university faculty across disciplines to collaborate with an Ed Tech student to improve an activity, assignment, or set of course materials in one of their courses for students to gain experience as instructional designers.

The SJE instructor saw this invitation as a great opportunity for an innovative approach to EDI education and agreed to participate. Although the instructor desired to develop ideas for incorporating more technology into the SJE course, the anxiety produced by a lack of technological expertise made this difficult. Teacher candidates in educator preparation programs are required to develop knowledge and skills in technology use and increase their ability to teach a diverse student population.

Two of the student-learning outcomes in the SJE course were to "critique systemic processes of discrimination in schools and schooling that marginalize and silence various groups of students and to apply theories of social justice education in the field." The hope was that this collaboration would allow the SJE instructor to help candidates develop their proficiency with EDI and technology by designing an assignment to evaluate candidates' development and to provide them with an opportunity to educate others about EDI. Thus, the SJE instructor was assigned a student from the EDT program.

The assigned student was a mid-career MA degree candidate in the Educational Technology program (EDT) who planned to make a career change into education. Despite some trepidation about the project, support and framing from the professor allowed the EDT student to see her prior experience as an asset even though it was not specifically in education.

The SJE instructor and the assigned EDT student met to discuss potential projects, agreeing on a new assignment designed to teach students how to design a one-minute PSA to promote the goals of EDI.

TECHNOLOGY: SUPPORTING SOCIAL JUSTICE EDUCATION

Social justice education (SJE) is an educational approach that examines how power and privilege are used in institutions to unintentionally and intentionally reproduce social inequality in society based on citizens' social group membership. SJE differs from diversity education in that the goal is to move students from awareness to action for social justice (Burrell Storms, 2014).

There are five principles of social justice education (Hackman, 2005). The first, content mastery, refers to EDI concepts and factual knowledge students need to understand how inequality operates in society. This information can help students recognize various forms of oppression at the micro and macro level.

The second and third principles—tools for critical analysis and personal reflection—encourage SJE instructors to help students engage in discernment about equity and social justice in schools and schooling. In addition, students are expected to question and challenge their own thinking, their classmates' ideas, and the information the instructor presents in the SJE classroom.

Tools for social action are an essential part of SJE. The main goal is for students to learn different processes for social change and how others have engaged in social action to combat oppression and promote EDI. One study found that students who learned about tools for social change felt more confident to engage in action taking (Burrell Storms, 2013). The last principle—awareness of multicultural group dynamics—highlights the importance of helping students build bridges across cultural differences in the classroom.

The PSA assignment created through this collaboration was intended to be an example of the principle "tools for social action" and provide students with the opportunity to apply their learning while educating others about the need for SJE in schools. This assignment taught students one form of social action engagement and allowed them to practice action taking in a safer environment before attempting this type of activity in their own classrooms. While the PSA functioned well within this education course, any course focused on SJE can incorporate this or similar assignments to promote EDI.

ASSIGNMENT DESCRIPTION

Public service announcements are typically thirty to sixty seconds and promote prosocial behavior toward a particular audience (Bator and Cialdini, 2000). PSAs can raise awareness, show the significance of a particular issue, give factual information, and encourage individuals to change their behavior (Bell, n.d., para. 2). They are made public to reach an audience using a variety of platforms, such as television or YouTube.

Smokey the Bear taught us, "Only you can prevent forest fires," while "A mind is a terrible thing to waste" was a successful PSA for the United Negro College Fund. In this case, the goal was to have teacher candidates persuade their audience to incorporate social justice education into their curriculum and schools.

The following assignment description was written in the syllabus: "The purpose of this assignment is for you to make an argument for multicultural education[1] in the form of a sixty second (one minute) public service announcement, or PSA. You can work alone or in teams (two to three). Your goal is to demonstrate your understanding of how schools and schooling can reproduce (or reduce) structural inequality and how social justice education can create equity for marginalized students. The PSA must be made public."

The assignment was due toward the end of the semester to give students time to learn EDI concepts, create a design, and write their scripts. Students decided where to post their PSAs. Facebook and YouTube were the most popular choices. They were required to share responses received about their PSAs during class time. This part of the assignment allowed the instructor and students to analyze the responses and make connections to course readings critically.

Most students were surprised they received any responses at all; however, they reported receiving both positive and negative responses from their audience. For example, one student shared how this activity forced a conversation with a close friend about promoting EDI. While this increased her confidence, she still felt anxiety about implementing this activity with her elementary-aged students because of the responses she might receive from parents. Discussion then turned to additional strategies that could help in this case.

WALKING STUDENTS THROUGH THE PROCESS

Adobe Spark Page and Spark Video were the tools recommended by the EDT instructor and consultant to show the SJE students how to create PSAs. These free online webpage and video-creation software applications are intuitive and user-friendly. Students were allowed to select any software to create their PSAs, but due to the ease of Adobe products, all students chose to use the Spark Page and Spark Video.

The EDT consultant designed a step-by-step process illustrating how to create a PSA. She included text and four short videos that included her voice, music, and pictures. When students clicked on the link, they saw a picture of a diverse group of people holding hands with the following title: "Creating a PSA to promote Multicultural Education." The assignment description immediately followed the title page.

The first video, "How to Get Started…," discussed deciding on the PSA focus, writing a script, timing the script, locating pictures and videos to use in the PSA, deciding which device to use (i.e., laptop, iPad, iPhone, etc.), and deciding which editing tool to use (e.g., Adobe Spark, WeVideo, etc.). The length of the video was fifty-eight seconds. Text describing PSAs, design ideas, and follow-up information to Video #1 was included as well.

Video #2 (fifty-seven seconds) walked students through the process of starting Adobe Spark, and Video #3 (one minute, twenty-one seconds) took them through the steps of designing their videos using the script or outline they created after watching Video #1. The consultant decided to use her eighty-four-year-old father in the video to illustrate the process! This was an effective way to encourage students who were apprehensive about the process. Once again, there was text included after each video that supported the information provided and gave additional ideas.

The final video (one minute, eight seconds) was all about editing. Once students completed the first draft of their project, the consultant provided additional ideas to encourage creativity. (The webpage and videos can be viewed at https://spark.adobe.com/page/NRMCBHqyZxpqP/.)

After the instructional site was complete, the link was included in the syllabus and in Blackboard.[2] Students could access the site at any time while working on their PSAs. The instructional site was shown during class to assess students' progress on the assignment and allow them time to ask the instructor questions and raise concerns.

EVALUATING THE PSAS

Collaborative assessment was used to determine the final criteria to be used to evaluate students' performance on the PSA. In small groups during class time, students were asked to develop five criteria to evaluate the PSAs. This exercise was implemented with the hope that students would gain more confidence and become more invested in the assignment (Falchikov, 2005). There was overlap for the criteria when each small group shared their recommendations.

The students and instructor reached consensus on the following criteria: (a) The PSA is within the time allotted; (b) the PSA is organized, and the message is clear and has good flow; (c) the message is creative and is told in unexpected or novel ways that grab the attention of the intended audience; (d) the argument for multicultural education is compelling, timely, and relevant to real-world issues, and it could motivate others to action; (e) and the PSA is an accurate and appropriate representation of multicultural education. After the criteria were selected, a holistic rubric was created using a point range for each. For example, for "the PSA is organized" criterion, students could receive a score between zero and seven.

Peer assessment was also used as part of the evaluation process. Each student was randomly assigned one PSA to score, as was the course instructor. Access to the assigned PSAs was provided via a link uploaded into Blackboard. All reviewers were encouraged to include comments to help authors understand why a particular score was given.

Grading is a major responsibility for future teachers, so peer assessment was a key part of the learning process. Students from any discipline can benefit from learning effective assessment and reporting techniques, however, so this is a skill that transfers across many professions. All students were required to submit their completed rubrics to the instructor electronically.

MOVING FORWARD

This was the first time this assignment was offered in the SJE course. Prior course assignments promoted EDI but did not require social action engagement. In this case, students both learned a new process to promote EDI and engaged in action taking, which the instructor found to be a significant change.

After reflecting on the overall process, the instructor plans to make the following changes. First, the instructor would create her own PSA as an example for students to illustrate the objectives of the assignment—social action engagement for equity, diversity, and inclusion in education. One of her teaching philosophies is never to ask students to do things you are unwilling to do yourself. Students need to see their instructors engaged in different forms of social action to encourage them to do the same. This practice would allow opportunities to help students with all facets of the assignment.

Second, one challenge about the collaboration was the consultant's (EDT student) availability during the summer before the SJE course was taught. Although the SJE instructor was technically the "client" in this case, it would have been helpful for the consultant to meet the students enrolled in the course beforehand to be accessible to them in case they had technical questions during the semester. The instructor for the "Creating and Curating Digital Course Materials" was available during the semester, however, and was more than willing to assist.

Third, this assignment was presented at the National Association for Multicultural Education International Conference in the fall of 2018. Feedback offered two suggestions that will be incorporated into the assignment requirements next time.

One suggestion was to add a written reflection piece to the assignment. Students engaged in class discussions about their PSAs but were not required to write about their experience. Asking students to reflect on social action engagement for multicultural education is a critical aspect of the process that was missed the first time.

A second suggestion was to conduct a follow-up study with candidates about this assignment. Students provided a few comments on the standardized evaluations given at the end of the semester. One student wrote that the PSA was creative, and another suggested that the rubric be created beforehand. A follow-up study would not only improve the assignment but also help the instructor understand what learning took place during the process and how this assignment informed their teaching about EDI.

CONCLUSION

Moving students from awareness to action is a challenging feat in a semester-long course. Asking students to complete assignments that reflect the social justice mission of the institution, however, is one way to teach students how to promote equity, diversity, and inclusion. Collaborating with colleagues who have expertise across disciplines was essential for this assignment to materialize. Seeking allies beyond your silo can be an exciting learning opportunity for faculty and students and necessary for working toward social change on campus and other communities.

NOTES

1. The concept of multicultural education is more common than social justice education; therefore, it was used in the assignment description.
2. The course management system used at the university.

REFERENCES

Alimo, C. (2012). From dialogue to action: The impact of cross-race intergroup dialogue on the development of white college students as racial allies. *Equity & Excellence in Education*, 45(1), 36–59.

Bator, R. J., and Cialdini, R. B. (2000). The application of persuasion theory to the development of effective proenvironmental public service announcements. *Journal of Social Issues*, 56(3), 527–41.

Bell, J. (n.d.). How to create the perfect public service announcement. Retrieved from http://www.govtech.com/education/news/How-to-Create-the-Perfect-Public -Service-Announcement.html.

Burrell Storms, S. (2014). Using social justice vignettes to prepare students for social action engagement. *Multicultural Perspectives*, 16(1), 1–7.

Burrell Storms, S. (2013). Preparing teachers for social justice advocacy: Am I walking my talk? *Multicultural Education*, 20(2), 33–39.

Conceptual Framework. (n.d.). Graduate School of Education and Allied Professions, Fairfield University.

Falchikov, N. (2005). *Improving assessment through student involvement: Practical solutions for aiding learning in higher and further education.* London: Routledge Falmer.

Gurin-Sands, C., Gurin, P., Nagda, B. A., and Osuna, S. (2012). Fostering a commitment to social action: How talking, thinking, and feeling make a difference in intergroup dialogue. *Equity & Excellence in Education*, 45(1), 60–79.

Hackman, H. (2005). Five essential components for social justice education. *Equity & Excellence in Education*, 38, 103–109.

Hartwell, E., Cole, K., Donovan, S., Greene, R., Burrell Storms, S., and Williams, T. (2017). Breaking down silos: Teaching equity, diversity, and inclusion across the disciplines, *Humboldt Journal of Social Relations*, 1(39), 143–62.

Morris, C. E. (2006). The archival turn in rhetorical studies; Or the archive's rhetorical (re)turn. *Rhetoric & Public Affairs*, 9(1), 113–115.

Chapter Six

Disturbing Voices: Literacy in the Archive and the Community

Betsy Bowen

"In most of us folks was the great desire to [be] able to read and write. We took advantage of every opportunity to educate ourselves."—John W. Fields, Layfayette, IN

"Lord, you'd better not be caught with a book in your hand. If you did, you were sold."—[paraphrased] Louisa Adams, Rockingham, NC

These are the words of two of the more than 2,300 formerly enslaved Americans interviewed by the Federal Writers' Project (FWP) between 1936 and 1938 as part of the effort to document American life. In these interviews, speakers talk about their lives during and after enslavement.

This chapter examines ways in which an English course on literacy and language can advance equity, diversity, and inclusion through a combination of archival research with the FWP interviews and community engagement. The course served sophomores at Fairfield University, a private institution in the Catholic Jesuit tradition, where 78 percent of the 4,000 full-time undergraduates are white, 2 percent are African American, and 7 percent are Hispanic (of any race) (2018–2019 Fact Book).

Together, they examined structural obstacles to literacy through archival research, using interviews with the last generation of Americans who were enslaved and through serving as literacy tutors in an elementary school where nearly 40 percent of students speak a language other than English at home and over 95 percent qualify for free or reduced-price lunch. Students in the course learned to listen to voices from the past and the present—voices that enriched and occasionally disturbed them.

In the process, they increased their self-awareness, learned about historical and contemporary structural forces that affect literacy, and put their knowledge into action through service to the community. This combination of archival research and contemporary engagement offers possibilities for courses in history, sociology, education, and other disciplines.

COURSE CONTEXT

Part of a general education program, "Literacy and Language" introduces students to literacy in American lives through fiction and nonfiction readings across a range of genres. Because the course satisfies Fairfield University's "U.S. Diversity" requirement, it has a particular responsibility to address issues related to equity, diversity, and inclusion (EDI). This responsibility influences the choice of literary works that are the foundation of the course.

Students read poems by Espaillat and Komunyakaa, as well as by Heaney and Wilbur. They hear spoken word poems by Lyiscott and other young poets. The choice of readings in other genres is similarly expansive: from Eaton's *The Children in Room E4,* a work of creative nonfiction that examines disparities in Connecticut's schools, to Shaw's classic *Pygmalion.*

Other aspects of the course also reflect its commitment to EDI. Students put their learning into action through literacy tutoring at a local elementary school. They reflect on their community engagement and course readings through low-stakes writing assignments in blogs or discussion boards and through a peer-led reflection session. They also do original archival research, reading interviews with the last generation of Americans who were enslaved. This chapter will trace the ways in which this combination of literary study, community engagement, and archival research can foster EDI, as well as the challenges that this work presents.

PREPARATION: FROM SELF TO OTHER

Einfeld and Collins (2008) distinguish awareness—"an individual's self-awareness and how cognizant they are of their own values, culture, and assumptions"—from knowledge—"an individual's content knowledge of other culture groups" (p. 101). The first section of the course is designed to help students cultivate both: that is, self-awareness about their formative experiences with literacy and also their knowledge about the experiences of others.

Students begin the course by reading contemporary personal narratives that focused on experiences with literacy and language, such as Tan's "Mother Tongue," Anzaldúa's "How to Tame a Wild Tongue," and Vuong's

"Surrendering." These readings prompt discussions of students' own experiences with literacy, language, and schooling—discussions that are often vivid, funny, or still prickly from long-remembered slights.

Next, students move to a broader consideration of literacy in American experiences, reading Brandt's (2001) "Accumulating Literacy." In it, Brandt traces experiences with literacy through four generations of a family, teasing out relationships between literacy, technology, economics, and social forces.

Students then conduct their own historical research, tracing experiences with literacy or language through three generations of a family and relating those experiences, as Brandt does, to the social and economic forces that influenced them. While students are not required to investigate their own families, most choose to do so, gaining greater awareness of the experiences and social forces that influenced their lives. As Mitchell (2008) notes, such exploration of identity, history, and experiences cultivate self-awareness, a prerequisite for authentic engagement with others.

LEARNING TO LISTEN TO VOICES FROM THE PAST

Literary works, no matter how imaginative and empathetic, offer a partial picture of American experiences with literacy. They are, necessarily, written by the literate. For much of this nation's history, however, many were denied access to literacy. The experiences of some of these Americans are available from oral histories collected by the Federal Writers' Project (FWP).

Now available through the Library of Congress, these interviews were part of a national effort to document American life through the words of those who experienced it. The FWP oral history project was, from its start, designed at least in part to correct the received understanding of history; Chief Editor B. A. Botkin maintained that, "To the white myth of slavery must be added the slaves' own folklore and folk-say of slavery" (Vol. 1, II, p. ix).

The decision to incorporate archival research into the course was motivated by a desire for a more inclusive and representative account of early African American literacy than excerpts from published narratives could provide. As Grobman (2017a) notes, oral history plays "a vital role in challenging the dominant narratives of American history and conventional sources of historical evidence" (120).

In earlier versions of the course, excerpts from Douglass' *Narrative of the Life of Frederick Douglass* and, occasionally, Harriet Jacobs' *Incidents in the Life of a Slave Girl* introduced students to ways in which African Americans had both sought and been denied opportunities for literacy in the nineteenth century. However, as published writers, Douglass and Jacobs are, by definition, not representative of the wide range of African Americans' experiences with literacy during the period.

More specifically, these oral histories collected from the last generation of enslaved Americans challenged students to consider historical precedents for contemporary disparities in education and to think critically about the laws and social systems that have contributed to those disparities (see Mitchell, 2008).

Archival projects of this kind, whether in History, American Studies, English, or other disciplines, enlarge students' understanding of lived experience in the past. The project described here is part of a larger "archival turn" (Morris, 2006) in rhetoric and composition, including projects that combine archival research and community engagement, such as Grobman (2017a and b) and Mutnick (2018).

During the past five years, through their research on accounts from the formerly enslaved, students have discovered stories of persistence, risk, achievement, and denial that illustrate the power attributed to literacy by both the enslaved and those who enslaved them. The accounts challenge both students' and instructor's ability to deal with emotionally charged material about race. Consequently, reading these oral histories calls on students to develop a variety of skills.

Hayden (2015) contends that "students learn to question the formation of history through such projects" (p. 406) because they engage with the complicated facts of historical experience that resist easy interpretation. Students' archival research became the foundation for "Reading Slavery, Writing Freedom," an interactive digital map that presents accounts of seeking, attaining, or being denied education with links to the original FWP transcripts.

Preparing students for the readings means attending to both the intellectual and affective contexts. Because the material is challenging and unfamiliar, students need to know why it is included in the course and how it contributes to their learning. Students also need to be forewarned about what they will encounter, particularly the use of phonetic spelling to render "dialect" in ways that reflect racist stereotypes.

Moreover, the narratives may disturb students, particularly students of color, because of racist terms used in the accounts and because of the horrors of slavery described. Students may feel angry, exposed, and/or isolated. The speakers themselves use terms that are highly charged and perhaps impossible to present in some contexts, even with disclaimers and careful framing. Certainly, teaching this material involves risk; in some contexts, the combination of racially charged terms and painful material might make the interviews too risky to consider. However, with support, students and faculty may both develop the interpersonal skills needed to manage this discomfort (Hartwell et al., 2017, p. 153).

Because archival research requires that students learn to read critically, with an awareness of the social and historical context, it is well-suited to courses in fields such as history and sociology that cultivate critical reading and awareness of social context. For instance, once students realize that the interviews were done in the period of Jim Crow and Ku Klux Klan (KKK) activity, often by white interviewers, with many speakers living in the area where they had previously been enslaved, they can more critically read interviews that express apparent nostalgia for slavery or refer to "good masters."

To prepare for this, students might roleplay situations in which they would be guarded if interviewed by a stranger about sensitive information, even in far less dangerous circumstances. Unless students have time and guidance to explore what might account for those descriptions, they may not be able to question or interpret what they encounter in the texts. An instructor might want to start with just a few accounts, preselected to represent a range of experiences with literacy and depictions of slavery. While that would sacrifice the opportunities for firsthand research, it would enable the instructor to anticipate challenges in the texts and provide more guidance to students as they encounter the material.

FROM KNOWLEDGE INTO ACTION

Courses committed to EDI seek to prepare students to use the self-awareness, knowledge, and skills they develop to act in the world (Hartwell et al., 2017). Students in this course did that by tutoring second graders at nearby Cesar A. Batalla Elementary School. There, students deal with the complexities of language, race, and power that they have seen presented in literary works from Shaw's *Pygmalion* to Lyiscott's spoken word poem on code-switching and the assumptions behind the word "articulate." Students prepare for the exploring characteristics of productive community engagement, as well as the implications of language used to describe it (Remen, 2017).

The American Association of Colleges and Universities identifies community engagement as a "high impact practice" that can increase student retention and engagement, when students have the opportunity both to "apply what they are learning in real-world settings and reflect in a classroom setting on their service experiences" (AAC&U). Service-learning is associated with increases in degree completion (Yue and Hart, 2017) and post-college civic engagement (Warchal and Ruiz, 2004).

DeLeon (2014) found that "intercultural service-learning leads to the development of students' intercultural skills as measured by the cultural intelligence action and strategy scores" and "can aid participants in developing intercultural skills, possibly even before awareness and knowledge are fully developed" (p. 26).

Nearly a decade ago, Stoecker, Tryon, and Hilgendorf (2009) identified the importance of "ongoing long-term commitment" and "intimate engagement" (p. 190) of university and community partners if service-learning or community engagement is to be effective. The Conference on College Composition and Communication expresses a similar caution, defining effective community engagement in the discipline as "well-conceived activities pursued over time to provide reciprocal benefits to both academic and community participants" and that create "discernible, specific contributions . . . to the public good" (CCCC).

The tutors in this course are part of a multi-year, multi-course partnership between Fairfield University and Cesar A. Batalla School. For the past six years, teachers from both institutions have met regularly to identify needs and develop programs. Based on that shared assessment of needs and assets, the partnership provides opportunities for university students to learn on-site.

The archival research on literacy and Eaton's contemporary account of schooling are useful here, reducing the risk that community-engagement unintentionally might reinforce the very social stereotypes it is designed to challenge (DeLeon, 2014; Green, 2003; Mitchell, 2008; Mitchell, Donahue, and Young-Law, 2012).

Mitchell (2008) contrasts what she describes as "traditional service-learning" that "emphasizes service without attention to systems of inequality" with "critical service-learning" that "is unapologetic in its aim to dismantle systems of injustice" (p. 50). Mitchell cautions that service-learning that does not consider the root causes of social problems "may involve students in the community in a way that perpetuates and reinforces an 'us-them' dichotomy" (p. 51), a situation that is especially likely when service-learning operates with a deficit model of communities (Mitchell, Donahue, and Young-Law, 2012).

REFLECTION

While research on service-learning is clear about the importance of reflection in service-learning, researchers disagree about whether reflection should primarily promote personal development (Hatcher, Bringle, and Muthiah, 2004) or "analysis of social inequities" (Einfeld and Collins, 2008). In their multi-campus study, Hatcher, Bringle, and Muthiah found that "the quality of the learning environment correlated most highly with the "integration of academic content" and the "nature of reflection activities" (p. 40). The most effective reflection activities are structured, regular, and designed to clarify personal values (p. 42).

By contrast, in a study of AmeriCorps participants, Einfeld and Collins (2008) emphasize the need for analysis of social inequities. They found that even intensive community engagement did not reliably lead participants to desire social change because "the educational focus and structured reflection of the program in this study were directed toward personal development" (p. 106). They suggest that instructors try other forms of reflection if they hope that reflection will encourage action.

In this course, students use a variety of forms of reflection. After the archival research, students write low-stakes reflections on their experience reading the accounts. Throughout their service-learning, students write a weekly blog or discussion posts, describing their experience of tutoring and reflecting on connections to other course material.

Occasionally, these short writing assignments reveal the kinds of resistance to service-learning that Jones and colleagues (2005) describe. In addition, at mid-semester, a Service-Learning Associate, a trained peer leader who has participated in the service-learning, leads a reflection session that incorporates individual responses and small-group discussion. To ensure that students speak freely, the instructor is not present.

CONCLUSION

In this course, students learn by examining literary texts, serving in the community, conducting archival research, and reflecting on those experiences. This combination of experiences affected some students in tangible ways. One reported that she registered to vote so that she could support public education; another wrote that he recognized his own family's experience in the accounts of slavery and valued that knowledge. Their reactions and those of others suggest that imaginative literature, historical accounts, and experiential education can help students develop a more expansive understanding of American experience.

REFERENCES

2018–2019 *Fact Book*. Office of Institutional Research. Fairfield University.

AAC&U, *High impact educational practices* https://www.aacu.org/leap/hips.

Anzaldúa, G. (2007). How to tame a wild tongue. *Borderlands/La frontera.* San Francisco: Aunt Lute Press.

Brandt, D. (2001). Accumulating literacy. In *Literacy in American Lives.* Cambridge: Cambridge University Press.

CCCC Statement on community-engaged projects in rhetoric and composition. Conference on College Composition and Communication, April 2016. http://cccc.ncte .org/cccc/resources/positions/community-engaged.

DeLeon, N. (2014). Developing intercultural competence by participating in intensive intercultural service-learning. *Michigan Journal of Community Service Learning,* 17–30.

Douglass, F. (2016). *Narrative of the life of Frederick Douglass* (2nd ed.). New York: W.W. Norton.

Eaton, S. (2009). *The children in room E4.* Chapel Hill, NC: Algonquin Books.

Einfeld, A., and Collins, D. (2008). The relationships between service-learning, social justice, multicultural competence, and civic engagement. *Journal of College Student Development,* 49(2), 95–109. 10.1353/csd.2008.0017.

Espaillat, R. P. *Bilingual-bilingüe.* Poetry Foundation. https://www.poetryfoundation .org/poems/46542/bilingual-bilingue.

Federal Writers' Project. *Slave narratives,* Volumes 1–17. Library of Congress. https://www.loc.gov/collections/slave-narratives-from-the-federal-writers-project -1936-to-1938/about-this-collection/.

Green, A. (2003). Difficult stories: Service-learning, race, class, and whiteness. *College Composition and Communication,* 55(2), 276–301. doi:10.2307/3594218.

Grobman, L. (2017a). Engaging race: Teaching critical race inquiry and community-engaged projects, *College English,* 80(2), 105–32.

Grobman, L. (2017b). Disturbing public memory in community writing partnerships. *College Composition and Communication,* 69(1), 35–60.

Hartwell, E. E., Cole, K., Donovan, S. K., Greene, R. L., Burrell Storms, S. L., and Williams, T. (2017). Breaking down silos: Teaching for equity, diversity, and inclusion across disciplines. *Humboldt Journal of Social Research,* 39, 143–62. Retrieved from http://digitalcommons.fairfield.edu/education-facultypubs/129.

Hatcher, J., Bringle, R., and Muthiah, R. (2004). Designing effective reflection: What matters to service-learning? *Michigan Journal of Community Service Learning,* 11, 38–46. http://hdl.handle.net/2027/spo.3239521.0011.104.

Hayden, W. (2015). Gifts of the archives. *College Composition and Communication,* 66(3), 402–26.

Heaney, S. *Digging.* Poetry Foundation. https://www.poetryfoundation.org/poems/47555/digging.

Jacobs, H. (2000). *Incidents in the life of a slave girl.* New York: Penguin Classics.

Jones, S., Gilbride-Brown, J., and Gasiorski, A. (2005). Getting inside the "underside" of service-learning: Student resistance and possibilities. In D. Butin (Ed.). *Service-learning in higher education: Critical issues and directions* (pp. 3–24). New York: Palgrave Macmillan.

Komunyakaa, Y. *My father's love letters.* Academy of American Poets. https://www .poets.org/poetsorg/poem/my-fathers-love-letters-audio-only.

Lyiscott, J. *Three ways to speak English*. TED Talk. https://www.ted.com/talks/jamila_lyiscott_3_ways_to_speak_english.

Mitchell, T. Donahue, D., and Young-Law, C. (2012). Service learning as a pedagogy of whiteness. *Equity and Excellence in Education*, 45(4), 612–29.

Mitchell, T. (2008). Traditional vs. critical service-learning. *Michigan Journal of Community Service Learning*, 14(2), 50–65.

Mutnick, D. (2018). Pathways to freedom: From the archives to the street. *College Composition and Communication*, 69(3), 374–401.

Reading slavery, writing freedom. Retrieved from: https://sites.google.com/student.fairfield.edu/readingslavery/home.

Remen, R. (August 6, 2017). Helping, fixing, or serving? *Lion's Roar*. https://www.lionsroar.com/helping-fixing-or-serving/.

Shaw, G. B. (1916; 2003). *Pygmalion*. New York: Penguin.

Stoecker, R., Tryon, E. A., and Hilgendorf, A. (2009). *The unheard voices: Community organizations and service learning*. Philadelphia: Temple University Press.

Tan, A. (1990). Mother tongue. *The Threepenny Review*, 43, 7–8.

Warchal, J., and Ruiz, A. (2004). The long term effects of undergraduate service-learning programs on postgraduate employment choices, community engagement and civic leadership. *New Perspectives in Service-Learning*. Information Age Publishing (pp. 87–106).

Wilbur, R. *The writer*. Academy of American Poets. https://www.poets.org/poetsorg/poem/writer/.

Vuong, O. (June 6 and 13, 2016). Surrendering. *The New Yorker*. https://www.newyorker.com/magazine/2016/06/06/ocean-vuong-immigrating-into-english.

Yue, H., and Hart, S. M. (2017). Service-learning and graduation: Evidence from event history analysis. *Michigan Journal of Community Service*, 24–41.

Part IV

AFFECTIVE CONSIDERATIONS

Chapter Seven

Awakening to Shame's Role in Privilege and Oppression

Kyle Forrest and Peter Thompson

A central challenge in addressing issues of equity, diversity, and inclusion (EDI) in the classroom is naming and working with shame. The challenge exists because shame acts behind the scenes to hold the structures of any group in place. When privilege and oppression are present, shame is the silent enforcer. To the extent that education is linked to social change, disregarding shame is no longer an option. Faculty need to awaken to how shame is operating in the classroom so that its inevitable effects are used to foster a liberating education rather than one that perpetuates privilege and oppression.

Faculty across disciplines will require training to work with shame, but there is no need for a formal research background in psychology or EDI work, just as learning a new technology does not require a computer science background. The work begins with faculty awakening to shame as it operates in themselves and then gaining experience to identify shame in the classroom. As faculty gain experience, they can assess the readiness of students for working with shame directly.

Naming shame may be particularly beneficial for EDI work to increase students' awareness of how shame is operating in themselves, in the classroom, and in society to perpetuate patterns of privilege and oppression. In this chapter, the authors will describe shame and provide an overview and examples of what working with shame looks like in the classroom.

DEFINING SHAME

Shame is a powerful and pervasive socializing force that operates at the relational level on the sense of self, arising when the self adjusts to an external standard that is not internally validated or is linked with self-rejection

(Yontef, 1997). It is a reaction to the lack of being received and is associated with a perception of the self as inadequate or unworthy. Shame is experienced intensely as an "emotional implosion"—an abrupt, discontinuous leap from the natural functioning of the self to feelings of high arousal, emotional distress, and cognitive confusion (Laing, 1960; Lewis, 1991; Lynde, 1958).

This is followed by self-relevant appraisals regarding violations of expectations (Tangney and Fischer, 1995). Although intense, shame can be situational, reasonable, appropriate, and socially useful as it motivates learning and a desire to change (Kelly and Lamia, 2018). If not handled with sufficient support, however, its effects can undermine confidence, decrease self-esteem, inhibit social interaction, and increase rigidity and defensiveness (Lewis, 1971; Yontef, 1997).

IDENTIFYING SHAME

In classrooms, raising awareness to difference, as in EDI work, will inevitably generate or trigger shame as it is present whenever privilege and oppression are operating, built into cultural, institutional, or group structures, and, not independently, into individual's perceptual and cognitive habits. Key to shame's operation is its characteristic feature of hiddenness as a "behind-the-scenes effect" (Weber and Gans, 2003, p. 382; Lewis, 1987) that internalizes the lack of reception and support as a function of the self's inherent inadequacy.

The self hides because there is a belief that if others knew of the inadequacy, they would leave. Critically important is that shame shifts responsibility for the inadequacy of support from the social world to the self, which is then assessed as being no good or unlovable, which is shameful.

Shame acts as internalized oppression, inhibiting natural curiosity and creative responses directed toward the true sources of oppression, both internally and externally through the unequal allocation of goods and symbolic capital that perpetuates systems of power.

What this means is that individuals' perceptions and evaluations of themselves, their bodies, beliefs, socioeconomic status, gender expression, and sexual orientation are inextricably embedded within—and a product of—a social world that denies the unequal distribution of support, goods, and symbolic capital (i.e., prestige, authority, etc.) as the foundation of legitimate power and natural privilege (see Bourdieu and Passeron, 1970/2000; Gramsci, 1971/2014; Foucault, 1980).

The authors argue this naturalizing tendency is a function of shame, and when it goes unidentified, shame acts as a core catalyst of privilege and oppression at the level of individual subjectivities.

In *Pedagogy of the Oppressed*, Paulo Freire (1970/2010) understood the liberating possibility of education was a function of individual epistemology.

> This task . . . [of humanist educators] implies [they] do not go to the people in order to bring them a message of "salvation," but in order to come to know through dialogue with them both their *objective situation* and their *awareness* of that situation (p. 95).

He says this process involves people becoming conscious of *how* they are viewing the world. "As they do this, they begin to see how they themselves acted while actually experiencing the situation they are now analyzing, and thus reach a 'perception of their previous perception'" (p. 115). Liberating individuals' perceptions and evaluations of themselves involves a process of gradually disentangling perception from its conditioned roots. The authors point to shame as the keystone in this disentangling process.

There is risk here because attempting to remedy oppression through a process that perpetuates shame is itself oppressive. Freire (1970/2010) understood this in the context of responding to social oppression by providing guidance for leaders of revolutionary causes to focus on process, discerning the difference between the cues of domination (i.e., conquest, divide and rule, manipulation, and cultural invasion) and liberating action (i.e., cooperation, unity for liberation, organization, and cultural synthesis).

Focusing on process is critical because, as Freire argued, all domination implies invasion, whether overt or camouflaged as helping. Without identifying shame, Freire is pointing to its guise, creating an image of the self's inadequacy while veiling its true source in inadequate support. Recognition of "intrinsic inferiority" by the invaded is key (Freire, 1970/2010, p. 153). Thus, naming and working with shame is critical to unveil this process.

STRATEGIES FOR THE CLASSROOM

Shame remains largely absent in the critical, contemplative, and anti-oppressive pedagogy literatures (see Darder et al., 2017; Barbezat and Bush, 2014; Berila, 2016). Even in psychology, shame was relatively neglected until the late 1980s. This has been attributed to the view of the self-dominated by classical Freudian individualist drive theory wherein self-reliance is viewed as mature and need as weak and shameful.

Further, shame marks dependency and, therefore, is weak and shameful in itself (Wheeler, 1995). In psychoanalysis, as the understanding of human nature moved to a relational, phenomenological, and field viewpoint, wherein the perception of reality is co-constructed by the self embedded in the field, the exploration of shame moved more into the foreground (Yontef, 1997). The understanding of shame shifted from an inward focus on the self and internal supports to a broader examination of the conditions of support in the environment (Wheeler, 1997).

The authors suggest integrating the work from the humanistic and existential branch of psychology on how to work with shame (for a distillation of the best of existential thought, see May, 1983). Contemplative pedagogy also has much to offer. The basic categories of these practices—communion, connection, and awareness (Barbezat and Bush, 2014)—echo the cues of liberating action set forth by Freire (1970/2010).

What is required is that shame move out of the shadows so that our "enchanted perception[s]" (Bourdieu, 2013, p. 298) can be recognized and explored with enough support and epistemological curiosity as essential elements of a liberating higher education. This will involve faculty honing intuitive discernment in themselves and their students through the potentially disruptive awareness of the "perception of their previous perception" (Freire, 1970/2010).

This way of working may represent a radical shift in how faculty perceive their pedagogy as it entails intuitive ways of knowing. The intuitively trained instructor is sensitive to the ways in which shame is present in a classroom. This requires instructors to be aware of how academic content is filtered through perceptual bias, including race, sexual orientation, gender expression, and social class.

Faculty must take into consideration how the likelihood of shame increases when the pedagogy is focusing too much on the instructor's agenda and not responding enough to the impact of predetermined structures on students. Generally, these impacts manifest in students as a behavioral or energetic shift away from active engagement with course material, of which instructors are more or less aware. The following section provides an overview of what bringing intuitive ways of working with shame into the classroom would entail.

While faculty traditionally foreground course content, such content, particularly when it involves EDI work, may be best learned when the didactic aspects of the content rests as background to be drawn upon selectively as it fits in the moment. Operating in the foreground is a deep awareness of an instructor's own perceptual filters or biases. This includes bringing awareness to representational figures or maps of the class as a group and working with how those interpretations may be clarifying or obscuring what is actually happening.

Faculty need not be put off by the messiness of what dynamically arises in interpersonal relationships. A critical aspect of this work is to sense, well enough, what kind of support each student may require to maintain an active and curious engagement with the material and how best to offer that support. To support another can be understood,

> as any element or collection of elements, internal or external, that make for the ability to proceed with a sense of integrity through an experience that is novel. That which preserves and encourages a person's felt integrity in the presence of new and thus challenging conditions can be taken as support to that person. (Lichtenberg, 1990, as quoted in Cole and Reese, 2018, p. 160).

Intuitively trained instructors are focused on and skilled in the relational as opposed to the individualistic; however, the individual is not invisible.

For example, that a student is, perhaps, the only Muslim in a class is held in awareness; nevertheless, the instructor pays abiding attention to how others in the class respond to this person and his/her/their worldview. The question is what will allow each student (and the instructor) to be curious about how privilege and oppression may be operating and any potential distortion of the academic material that occurs as a result.

Intuitive instructors are concerned with what is taking place moment-to-moment in the classroom, including knowing the difference between using the language of domination as opposed to the language of difference. The language of domination assumes or commands a shared perspective and exploits the internal oppression of shame through confluence to the authority view. The language of difference is attuned and responsive, knowing that much is said by the body, by posture and physical tension—and these ways of communicating need to be listened for and heard.

As examples, faculty may notice resistance or interruptions of energetic movement in the classroom, including overachieving, underachieving, erratic attendance (particularly when it seems to be affecting the group), prolonged silence, anger, hypercritical behavior, distancing, and facial and body expressions of disgust, all of which are shame-based. Each or a combination of several will serve to diminish the energy in the room, creating a sense of stagnation or boredom, and generate additional shame-based, shame-creating behavior.

The concrete strategies employed by the intuitively trained instructor are endless in variety but might be categorized as natural or formal. The natural strategy is designed creatively in the moment from sensing what might be immediately helpful. If a number of students are struggling with a poem's meaning, the instructor might ask students to select one word or phrase from the poem that grabs their attention, sit with those words—repeating them internally—and listening to what arises. A formal strategy is created outside the immediate experience of the classroom but grounded in it.

This difference may be subtle, but here, the reason for the exercise does not emerge from what is arising in the moment. For example, the instructor might devote a class to having students work in pairs with poems each has selected. One student would read his/her/their poem while the other listens, and both would allow themselves to have whatever experience the reading evokes.

These two strategies contrast with a more ungrounded approach that uses a predetermined structure that is less informed by what the students may need to support their curious engagement. This is one scenario in which faculty would ask students to focus on particular lines in a given poem, ones that speak more to the illustrative purposes of the instructor rather than what might engage the natural curiosity of students.

If ungrounded practice is characteristic of pedagogy, those students for whom this approach is effective would be privileged, and others, for whom this approach was less accessible, are left with the residue of inadequate support—shame. What is most effective in helping students learn are strategies that are informed by an intuitive understanding of how support, as defined earlier, works in this particular group. Some resistances must be dealt with in private. Any repeated, intense emotion from one student would need to be addressed individually.

Resistances that more obviously relate to the entire group, such as a continuing drop of energy in the room reflected in students looking away, not responding to, or challenging the material before understanding what it entails, can be addressed openly by stating that awareness—"I notice . . . what do you make of that . . . ?" Here, the noticing becomes a question posed to the students rather than a problem to be fixed, judged, or denied.

FEELING STUCK

There will be moments when an instructor feels stuck. Getting stuck occurs all the time in classrooms, and these places of being stuck present *the* opportunity for teaching. As an individual or a group is helped to loosen the stuck places without judgment or force, the possibility for transformative learning occurs as new behavior, whether intellectual or interpersonal (and probably both), takes place naturally.

For example, if oppression is at the core of course material, the instructor may sense tension arising in the classroom. Instead of minimizing or avoiding this tension, the instructor may help students loosen and take advantage of this as a place to explore a novel experience. With faculty that are more experienced, introducing and identifying shame as an inevitable aspect of learning assists to normalize the experience of shame and open curiosity to the process.

The instructor might choose to use a contemplative practice of slowing things down, suggesting students move inwardly with awareness, paying attention to breathing, tension in the body, and asking students to breathe a bit more and explore any tension. As students become more comfortable with this approach and physically settle—becoming more present—the instructor might then introduce an experiment involving the academic material such as "Imagine a time in your life when you felt stifled, pushed down . . . paying attention to how you felt, how your body felt, what you were thinking . . ."

In working with the body, faculty need to be mindful that some students likely have trauma histories. Offering alternative practices allows students to self-select which practice(s) would feel more engaging. Opening up a variety of ways to share experience—in reflective writing, artistic form, in pairs, and/or opening discussion with a larger group—is grounded in the understanding that what may feel supportive for one student may not feel supportive for another.

CONCLUSION

The difference between a liberating education and one that perpetuates privilege and oppression depends on helping students awaken to their conditioned ways of perceiving and organizing experience. This process inevitably raises shame.

The authors believe a process pedagogy that actively works with shame as it unfolds in the classroom is *the* natural next step toward which the critical, contemplative, and anti-oppressive literatures are pointing. Without this work, addressing equity, diversity, and inclusion in higher education risks reproducing what it seeks to liberate by confusing what it prefers with what is.

REFERENCES

Barbezat, D. P., and Bush, M. (2014). *Contemplative practices in higher education.* San Francisco: John Wiley & Sons.

Berila, B. (2016). *Integrating mindfulness into anti-oppression pedagogy: Social justice in higher education.* New York: Routledge.

Bourdieu, P. (2013). Symbolic capital and social classes. *Journal of Classical Sociology*, 13(2), 292–302.

Bourdieu, P., and Passeron, J. (1970/2000). *Reproduction in education, society, and culture* (2nd ed.). London: Sage.

Cole, P., and Reese, D. (2018). *New directions in gestalt group psychotherapy: Relational ground, authentic self.* New York: Routledge.

Darder, A., Torres, R. D., and Baltodana, M. P. (Eds.) (2017). *The critical pedagogy reader* (3rd ed.). New York: Routledge.

Foucault, M. (1980). *Power: Knowledge.* New York: Vintage Books.

Freire, P. (1970/2010). *Pedagogy of the oppressed.* New York: Continuum International Publishing.

Gramsci, A. (1971/2014). *Selections from the prison notebooks.* New York: International Publishers.

Kelly, V. C., and Lamia, M. C. (2018). *The upside of shame: Therapeutic interventions using the positive aspects of a "negative" emotion.* New York: W.W. Norton & Co.

Laing, R. (1960). *The divided self.* Chicago: Quadrangle.

Lewis, H. B. (1971). *Shame and guilt in neurosis.* New York: International Universities Press.

Lewis, H. B. (1987). *The role of shame in symptom formation.* Hillsdale, MI: Erlbaum.

Lewis, M. (1991). *Shame: The exposed self.* New York: The Free Press.

Lichtenberg. P. (1990). *Community and confluence: Undoing the clinch of oppression.* New York: Peter Lang.

Lynde, H. (1958). *On shame and the search for identity.* New York: Harcourt, Brace & Co.

May, R. (1983). *The discovery of being: Writings in existential psychology.* New York: W.W. Norton & Co.

Owen-Smith, P. (2018). *The contemplative mind in the scholarship of teaching and learning.* Bloomington: Indiana University Press.

Tangney, J., and Fischer, K. W. (1995). *Self-conscious emotions: The psychology of shame, guilt, embarrassment, and pride.* New York: Guilford Press.

Weber, R. L., and Gans, J. S. (2003). The group therapist's shame: A much undiscussed topic. *International Journal of Group Psychotherapy*, 53(4), 395–416.

Wheeler, G. (1995). Shame in two paradigms of therapy. *British Gestalt Journal*, 4, 76–85.

Wheeler, G. (1997). Self and shame: A gestalt approach. *Gestalt Review*, 1(3), 221–44.

Yontef, G. (1997). Relationship and sense of self in gestalt therapy training. *Gestalt Journal*, 20(1), 17–48.

Chapter Eight

Know Thyself:
Implicit Bias and Mindfulness

Paula Gill Lopez

This chapter describes how teachers who practice mindfulness will be better equipped to help students deeply engage with equity, diversity, and inclusion (EDI) issues. The first section defines mindfulness and implicit bias and describes their points of intersection using a neuroscience lens. The second section describes specific mindful awareness practices (MAPS) that can be used by EDI instructors to enhance their own self-awareness, knowledge, skill, and behavior before asking students to engage in conversations related to EDI.

MINDFULNESS AND IMPLICIT BIAS

The discussion of implicit bias and mindfulness has neuroscience at its core. Fiske and others (Amodio, 2014; Fiske, 2013; Powell, 2015a) have conceived of modern-day prejudice as something different from the overt prejudice and discrimination of past generations borne out of isolation and ignorance. They maintain that much of today's racism is driven by unconscious cognitive biases—implicit bias.

Implicit bias is inherently rooted in the brain's mission to survive at any cost. Early in human evolution, the reptilian portion of the brain scanned the world for danger. The danger could be predators or members of another group who were competitors for food, mates, land, and so on. To this day, when danger (or any strong emotion) is detected, the amygdala releases stress hormones into the body, causing an increase of blood flow to our extremities in preparation to fight, flee, or freeze (e.g., play dead).

Implicit bias can be conceived of as a primitive response to a threat outside of the immediate tribe or community. Fear of the "other" is hardwired into our brains for survival. For this reason, addressing racism on a conscious level alone is often not effective (Amodio, Devine, and Harmon-Jones, 2008; Harris and Fiske, 2006; Powell, 2015a).

Human brains have grown and evolved for higher-order thinking. The prefrontal cortex has emerged as the rational, decision-making part of the brain (among other functions) and has neuroplasticity, which is the ability of the brain to adapt and change (Davidson and Begley, 2012; Hölzel et al., 2009).

As a result, new neural pathways can be created to bring implicit bias out of the shadows into the light of consciousness, where it can be addressed in a deliberate, proactive, and ongoing way. While there are multiple techniques, frameworks, and strategies for doing this type of EDI work on a conscious level, this chapter is focused on how to prepare the mind to engage in that work. Enter mindfulness.

Mindfulness is defined as bringing nonjudgmental, focused attention to whatever is being experienced in the present moment (Kabat-Zinn, 2003). In the last decade, researchers discovered a host of beneficial outcomes that occur from practicing mindfulness meditation. Mindful awareness practices (MAPS) have research outcomes that directly address symptoms of implicit bias, including mitigating fear and anxiety, promoting greater awareness of self and others, and interconnectedness (Murphy-Shigematsu, 2018).

Simply put, mindfulness helps to address prejudiced and biased behavior in adults by calming the amygdala's response to those who are unconsciously perceived as different and allowing the brain to burn and access new neural pathways of self-awareness, self-regulation, and compassion (Davidson and Begley, 2012; Hopthrow, Hooper, Mahmood, Meier, and Weger, 2017; Lueke and Gibson, 2015; Magee, 2016; Murphy-Shigematsu, 2018; Stell and Farsides, 2016).

Mindfulness does not address implicit bias directly but rather works on an unconscious neural level. MAPS can be used with people of any age across disciplines. In a college classroom, MAPS can assist a professor who is preparing to investigate her own implicit biases and become a role model for greater self-awareness, helping to create the ideal conditions for helping students explore and uncover their own implicit biases.

MAPS TO INCREASE SELF-AWARENESS AND EXPOSE IMPLICIT BIAS

When discussing implicit bias, Powell maintains, "To keep it going, it only needs a lack of self-awareness" (Powell, 2015b). Similar to those who have identified self-awareness as a necessary learning objective for EDI, there is consensus among researchers who study implicit bias that self-awareness is a necessary component of any intervention designed to address it (Amodio, Devine, and Harmon-Jones, 2008; Amodio and Swencionis, 2018; Devine, 1989; Fiske, 2013).

Self-awareness is one of two primary outcomes of MAPS; the other is self-regulation (Hölzel et al., 2009). In this section, specific MAPS are described that can prepare the way for EDI learning on two levels: (1) the instructor's own mindfulness practice and its effect on the classroom and (2) using MAPS with students in the classroom.

Instructor's Mindfulness Practice

There is currently a solid body of literature attesting to the wide-ranging benefits of mindfulness for instructors (for instance, see Emerson et al., 2017). Mindfulness has its origins in thousands of years of religious tradition but has exploded into the secular mainstream over the last decade. Mindfulness can be learned in multiple ways, including formal training, organized retreats, and simply by focusing attention at the moment without aids or by using free guided meditations found on websites, YouTube videos, and mobile apps.

Jon Kabat-Zinn's *Mindfulness-Based Stress Reduction* (MBSR) program is one of the most popular evidence-based trainings. It is taught by a certified MBSR teacher, most often in an eight-week format, but it can also be found in a more condensed format, such as a five- or seven-day retreat. The MBSR program has three components: (1) didactic, (2) experiential, and (3) reflective. Dave Potter, a certified MBSR trainer, put the eight-week course online. The course can be accessed at the following link for free: https://palousemindfulness.com/index.html.

Mindfulness retreats are a good way to be immersed in a mindfulness experience. There are programs for beginners and programs for experienced practitioners. The Center for Contemplative Mind in Society (https://www.contemplativemind.org) is an organization whose primary focus is higher education. It was founded in 1997 and coordinates and sponsors numerous events, including conferences, retreats, lectures, intensive workshops, and so on. The organization seeks "to recast the traditional foundations for education into a truly integrative, transformative, and communal enterprise that is wholly open and inclusive of all backgrounds" (retrieved from: https://www.contemplativemind.org/about).

People can also practice mindfulness without formal training. One only has to bring focused attention to the present moment, without judgment (Kabat-Zinn, 2003). This can be accomplished through the use of anchors (any of the five senses, body sensations, emotions, or thoughts). The anchor most often used is breath. A basic introduction for breathing meditation can be found at the following link: https://smithcenter.org/wp-content/uploads/files/down loads/mindful-breathing-meditation.pdf.

The Mindful Awareness Research Center (MARC) at UCLA was founded in 2004 and hosts a website (https://www.uclahealth.org/marc/mindful-med-itations) that offers an excellent array of free guided meditations, including body scans; breathing meditation; and breath, body, and sound meditation. The body scan is a common meditation practice in which the practitioner notices different parts of the body one by one, softening and releasing any tension found there. A short three-minute guided body scan can be found at: https://www.uclahealth.org/marc/mpeg/Body-Scan-Meditation.mp3.

Researchers have recently begun to examine different types of mindful-ness and have found they yield different outcomes (Kok and Singer, 2017a; Sauer-Zavala, Walsh, Eisenlohr-Moul, and Lykins, 2013). Several studies have identified loving kindness meditation (LKM) as being most effective in ameliorating implicit bias because of its focus on acceptance and love (Kang, Gray, and Dovidio, 2015; Stell and Farsides, 2016).

The LMK "aims to self-regulate an affective state of unconditional kind-ness toward the self and others" by wishing good things—health, happiness, kindness, strength, and so on—to the self, others, and the world (Stell and Farsides, 2016, pp. 140–41). An example of the loving kindness guided medi-tation can be found at: https://www.uclahealth.org/marc/mpeg/05_Loving _Kindness_Meditation.mp3.

MAPS are easily learned, practiced, and customized to individual pref-erences (Davidson and Begley, 2012; Kok and Singer, 2017a). Even brief MAPS have been found to decrease the anxiety that can lead to prejudiced behaviors (Lueke and Gibson, 2015; Stell and Farsides, 2016). The bottom line is that the positive outcomes associated with practicing mindfulness can be obtained informally by bringing focused attention to any daily task and being fully immersed in a deep sensory experience (Gill-Lopez, 2019).

Educators practicing mindfulness can employ it in the classroom as they set up for discussions related to EDI. For example, using mindfulness, educators can model a calm, self-regulated presence for students' nervous systems to involuntarily emulate. The parasympathetic nervous system of young adults is completed through the unconscious attunement to significant adults in their environment (Hatfield, Cacioppo, and Rapson, 1993). When educators are calm, students are more likely to allow themselves to be vul-nerable. Vulnerability is an essential component for productively uncover-ing, examining, and coming to terms with difficult feelings that can arise from EDI discussions.

Using MAPS with Students

To cultivate mindful awareness in the classroom, begin class with a mindful moment. Simply instructing students to pay attention to an anchor—their breath, sounds in the room, body sensations, and so on—for one to three minutes can strengthen focused attention. Listening to a short recorded guided meditation accomplishes the same thing.

Another brief grounding activity instructs students to close their eyes or lower their gaze and take a moment to identify one word that describes how they are feeling in the moment. The 4-7-8 breathing technique guides students to take deep breaths on the instructor's count—inhale for four counts, hold for seven seconds, and exhale for eight seconds, resulting in a calm state. An exercise like this can be especially important after an intense conversation related to EDI.

Cultivating understanding between students can be central to discussions related to EDI. MAPS can lay the groundwork for understanding by asking students to engage in activities in class in which they share information about themselves. While sharing information alone is not necessarily engaging EDI, this helps set the right tone between students before they engage in EDI discussions.

Kok and Singer (2017b) studied the effects of contemplative dyads and found that knowledge about their partner, obtained through affective dyad exercises, increased feelings of closeness to and acceptance of the partner. The exercises can increase perspective, essentially reclassifying people from the "other" or out-group to the "in-group" (van Bavel, Packer, and Cunningham, 2008). Teachers can simulate these mindfulness dyads with pair-and-share in-class exercises.

One example of a dyadic pair-and-share is where each student takes turns being the speaker and the listener. The speaker shares a high (a gratitude-eliciting situation) and a low (a challenging situation) of the past week, describing the corresponding feelings and body sensations of each. The listener does not respond, either verbally or nonverbally, but instead attends to the speaker's stories in an active, empathic way (Kok and Singer, 2017b). Other sample prompts to stimulate mindful dyadic speaking and listening designed are as follows:

- Name one stressor and one thing you do daily to relieve stress.
- Share something you learned about yourself from this class.
- Share something you have applied from this class.
- Share your biggest challenge in this class.
- Share a value that has guided you in your life. Who did you learn this value from?

- Pick a paper (from a jar full of paper slips with emotions written on them). Share a time when you experienced the emotion.

Students engage in these activities before a discussion about issues related to EDI since this primes them to have a more respectful and attuned discussion.

While the aforementioned examples pertain more to preparing students for conversations related to EDI, a final example suggests how MAPS are connected to EDI conversations. Magee (2016), a law professor at the University of San Francisco, developed the ColorInsight Meditation, which she uses to assist her law students in developing self-awareness to reveal race and other forms of social identity–based bias they experience. Magee walks students through this meditation:

> Sit in silence for a few minutes. Think back on your life experiences over the past twenty-four hours with nonjudgmental awareness. Reflect on the settings in which you have moved, including to, from, and during work. What races do you typically encounter? In what roles? Do some groups predominate as among the powerful or the powerless? Take a few minutes to write in a journal about what you know, including the habits or conditioning you may have around acknowledging or avoiding this aspect of your own life experience. Notice not only the thoughts but also emotions and physical sensations that arise as you seek to turn more forthrightly to this aspect of your own life. Consider developing an intention of gently bringing mindful awareness to these aspects of your life, inviting the will to work with dimensions of your experience with greater compassion, courage and curiosity in the coming week (p. 27).

Magee's meditation demonstrates how to blend the calming practice of mindfulness with direct questions related to EDI.

The outcome is an opportunity for students to reflect as they journal about race, power, and social conditioning from within the safe space created by the MAPS. As a skilled facilitator in EDI issues, Magee could then leverage this exercise into a productive conversation with her law school students about how race, power, and social conditioning might affect their interactions with future clients.

CONCLUSION

Of course, any of the mindfulness practices described in the instructor's MAPS section detailed in this chapter can be used with students for a few minutes at the beginning of class to promote greater self-awareness and nonjudgmental acceptance. While this chapter primarily focuses on what MAPS are and how they work as preparation for EDI discussions, trained instructors can decide how best to incorporate these techniques into their classroom discussions about difficult topics.

REFERENCES

Amodio, D. M., and Swencionis, J. K. (2018). Proactive control of implicit bias: A theoretical model and implications for behavior change. *Journal of Personality and Social Psychology,* 115(2), 255–75. doi: 10.1037/pspi0000128.

Amodio, D. (2014). The neuroscience of prejudice and stereotyping. Nature Reviews. *Neuroscience,* 15(10), 670–82. doi:10.1038/nrn3800.

Amodio, D. M., Devine, P. G., and Harmon-Jones, E. (2008). Individual differences in the regulation of intergroup bias: The role of conflict monitoring and neural signals for control. *Journal of Personality and Social Psychology,* 94(1), 60–74. doi: 10.1037/0022-3514.94.1.60.

Davidson, R. J., and Begley, S. (2012). *The emotional life of your brain: How its unique patterns affect the way you think, feel, and live—and how you can change them.* New York: New American Library.

Devine, P. G. (1989). Stereotypes and prejudice: Their automatic and controlled components. *Journal of Personality and Social Psychology,* 56, 5–18, http://dx.doi.org/10.1037/0022-3514.56.1.5.

Emerson, L. M., Leyland, A., Hudson, K., Rowse, G., Hanley, P. and Hugh-Jones, S. (2017). Teaching mindfulness to teachers: a systematic review and narrative synthesis, *Mindfulness,* 8(5), 1136–49. doi: 10.1007/s12671-017-0691-4.

Fiske, S. T. (2013). *Social cognition.* Los Angeles: SAGE.

Gill-Lopez, P. (2019). Self-care: Mind-body best practice. In M. A. Bray and C. Maykel (Eds.) *Promoting Mind–Body Health in Schools: Interventions for Mental Health Professionals.* Washington, DC: American Psychological Association.

Harris, L. T., and Fiske, S. T. (2006). Dehumanizing the lowest of the low: Neuroimaging responses to extreme out-groups. Psychological Science, 17(10), 847–53. doi: 10.1111/j.1467-9280.2006.01793.x.

Hatfield, E., Cacioppo, J. T., and Rapson, R. L. (1993). *Emotional contagion.* New York: Editions de la Maison des sciences de l'homme.

Hölzel, B. K., et al. (2009). Stress reduction correlates with structural changes in the amygdala. *Social Cognitive and Affective Neuroscience,* 5(1), 11–17.

Hopthrow, T., Hooper, N., Mahmood, L., Meier, B. P., and Weger, U. (2017). Mindfulness reduces the correspondence bias. *The Quarterly Journal of Experimental Psychology,* 70(3), 351–60. doi: 10.1080/17470218.2016.1149498.

Kabat-Zinn, J. (2003) Mindfulness-Based Interventions in Context Past, Present, and Future. *Clinical Psychology Science and Practice,* 10, 144–56.

Kang, Y., Gray, J., and Dovidio, J. (2015). The head and the heart: Effects of understanding and experiencing lovingkindness on attitudes toward the self and others. *Mindfulness,* 6(5), 1063–70. doi:10.1007/s12671-014-0355-6.

Kok, B. E., and Singer, T. (2017a). Phenomenological fingerprints of four meditations: Differential state changes in affect, mind-wandering, meta-cognition, and interception before and after daily practice across 9 months of training. *Mindfulness*, 8(1), 218–31.

Kok, B. E., and Singer T. (2017b). Effects of contemplative dyads on engagement and perceived social connectedness over 9 months of mental training: A randomized clinical trial. *JAMA Psychiatry,* 74(2):126–34. doi:10.1001/jamapsychiatry.2016.3360.

Lueke, A., and Gibson, B. (2015). Mindfulness meditation reduces implicit age and race bias: The role of reduced automaticity of responding. *Social Psychological and Personality Science*, 6(3), 284–91. doi: 10.1177/1948550614559651.

Magee, R. V. (2016). Reacting to racism: Mindfulness has a role in educating lawyers to address ongoing issues. *ABA Journal*, 102(8), 26–27.

Murphy-Shigematsu, S. (2018). *From mindfulness to heartfulness: transforming self and society with compassion* (First edition.). Oakland, CA: Berrett-Koehler Publishers, Inc.

Powell, J. P. (2015a). *Racing to justice: Transforming our conceptions of self and other to build an inclusive society*. Bloomington: Indiana University Press.

Powell, J. P. (May 19, 2015b). Understanding our new racial reality starts with the unconscious. Retrieved from https://greatergood.berkeley.edu/article/item/understanding_our_new_racial_reality_starts_with_the_unconscious.

Sauer-Zavala, S.E., Walsh, E.C., Eisenlohr-Moul, T.A., and Lykins, E. L. B. (2013). Comparing mindfulness-based intervention strategies: Differential effects of sitting meditation, body scan, and mindful yoga. *Mindfulness* 4, 383. https://doi.org/10.1007/s12671-012-0139-9.

Stell, A. J., and Farsides, T. (2016). Brief loving-kindness meditation reduces racial bias, mediated by positive other-regarding emotions. *Motivation and Emotion*, 40(1), 140–47. doi: 10.1007/s11031-015-9514-x.

van Bavel, J. J., Packer, D. J., and Cunningham, W. A. (2008). The neural substrates of in-group bias: A functional magnetic resonance imaging investigation. *Psychological Science*, 19(11), 1131–39. doi: 10.1111/j.1467-9280.2008.02214.x.

Chapter Nine

Transforming Fear into Courage: EDI and Compassion-Based Learning

Josephine Wong and Carla Hilario

Transformative learning in higher education has been identified as the key to individual and collective empowerment for social change (Kroth and Cranton, 2014). The objectives of this chapter are twofold: (1) introduce Acceptance and Commitment to Empowerment (ACE) as an approach to transformative learning; and (2) illustrate the selected application of ACE-based learning principles and activities to promote dialogue, reflexivity, and commitment toward social justice, equity, diversity and inclusion (SJ-EDI) among university students in nursing and allied health/social-care disciplines.

ACE FOR TRANSFORMATIVE LEARNING

Acceptance and Commitment to Empowerment (ACE) is a compassion-based integrated model of transformative learning that was developed for use with community-based action research to promote psychological flexibility, reduce stigma, and encourage collective action for social justice (Li, Fung, Maticka-Tyndale, and Wong, 2017; Li and Wong, 2016). ACE is innovative in that it combines learning strategies that connect learners at the intrapersonal and interpersonal levels. ACE draws on the following concepts and processes (see also Figure 9.1):

- Two value-guided principles and processes—"compassion" based on deep listening, understanding, and loving-kindness (Nhất Hạnh, 1997; hooks, 2000), and "interbeing," or interconnectedness (i.e., each individual is part of the whole web of life) (Nhất Hạnh, 2003).
- Six psychological processes from acceptance and commitment therapy (ACT)[1]

- to promote psychological flexibility—"mindfulness" (being present); "self-as-context" (observer self); "acceptance" (of internal struggle; i.e., wanted and unwanted thoughts and feelings); "cognitive defusion" (deliteralization of thoughts, letting go of labels and problematic rules); "values" (what matters); and "committed action" (guided by chosen values) (Hayes, Strosahl, and Wilson, 1999)
- Four collective empowerment processes based on Freire's critical pedagogy (1970/2000) and Heron's experiential learning (1996)—"critical reflection," "critical dialogue," "experiential learning," and "collaborative learning."

APPLICATION OF ACE IN TRANSFORMATIVE LEARNING

Within the ACE approach, teachers and students are co-learners who recognize that this relationship is constrained by institutional expectations of course requirements, approved curriculum standards, and performance

Figure 9.1. The ACE Model.

measures. Going beyond conventional methods of learning that privilege cognitive analysis and scholarly writing, ACE-based learning strategies engage co-learners in critical pedagogical processes and experiential learning that support them to reconnect to their emotional and spiritual being.

The two overarching principles and processes that are critical in SJ-EDI education are "interbeing" and "compassion," which promote nonviolent and engaged activism (Fernandes, 2003). The word "interbeing" or *tiep hien* (in Vietnamese) was coined by Zen Buddhist scholar and teacher Thich Nhất Hạnh (1987). *Tiep hien* means being in touch with the reality of the world here and now while continuing on a path of relational learning and engaged practice.

The notion of interbeing captures the essential interconnectedness of the universe and the interdependence of all beings. Since there is not a separate independent self, our action and nonaction affect not only ourselves but all other beings (Nhất Hạnh, 2003). Interbeing is an important concept that is increasingly taken up by scholars and activists working toward social and environmental justice to counter neoliberalism and structural violence (Asher, 2003; Grigg and Tidwell, 2015; Wang, 2017).

"Compassion," derived from the word *karuna* (Sanskrit and Pali), refers to "the desire to ease the pain of another person" and having "the ability to do so" (Nhất Hạnh, 1997, p. 3). Compassion can be deepened through the practice of mindfulness, which enables the co-learners to develop concentration, awareness, and insights. Evidence indicates that mindfulness is effective in reducing anxiety and fear and promoting interpersonal relationships (Hofmann, Sawyer, Witt, and Oh, 2010).

However, integrating the notions of interbeing and compassion in SJ-EDI is often challenging when the education systems in Canada and other Western societies with diverse populations only recognize Western knowledge as legitimate and valid (Singh, Manathunga, Bunda, and Jing, 2016). Many educators and students shy away from Indigenous and "non-Western" knowledge except when these knowledges and philosophies have been appropriated, adapted, and claimed as Western knowledge (Harding, 2011).

APPLYING ACE IN SJ-EDI EDUCATION

The following sections consist of exemplars of ACE-based learning strategies based on the authors' experiences in integrating SJ-EDI education into the courses they taught in nursing and allied health-/social-care disciplines. Description of these strategies is organized based on the pedagogical processes outlined in the ACE model.

Strategy 1: Co-constructing a Relational Space for Learning

Creating a "safe" space for learning has become a dominant discourse in higher education. Since the classroom is not insulated from the external world, it is impossible to create an absolutely "safe" space for co-learners. The discourse of safe space often contributes to political correctness and inadvertently reinforces white privileges and domination, whereby students of marginalized identities bear the burden of explanations about inequities (Martinez-Cola et al., 2018).

A more effective strategy is to co-construct a "relational space" that acknowledges the lived experiences of all co-learners and also the structural contexts of these lived experiences. A relational space for SJ-EDI education, in Canada as a white-settler society, can be created through:

- Guiding principles—In the first class, the instructor names upfront the goals and objectives of the course; the institutional expectations about the roles and responsibilities of the students and instructors; and invites all co-learners to create a set of agreed-upon principles to guide their interactions and communication throughout the course. These guiding principles are revisited at each class to promote commitment to value-guided interactions. Co-learners can refer to these principles when conflicts arise, and discussions become intense.
- Land acknowledgment—Each class begins with an acknowledgment that co-learning is taking place on Indigenous land. This acknowledgment is a relational strategy that enables co-learners to connect to the often denied historical and ongoing colonial practices that implicate everyone in the class. It is also a reminder of everyone's individual and collective responsibilities in correcting the existing injustices experienced by Indigenous peoples and protecting the Earth.
- Mindfulness practice—Co-learners engage in a mindfulness exercise at the beginning of each class and also after an intense and emotional discussion. By providing relevant resources on mindfulness, co-learners are invited to take turns in leading the mindfulness exercises, which support everyone to practice the art of being fully present, reclaiming their body-mind-spirit connections, (re)connecting to their compassion for self and others, and accepting their fears and feelings of vulnerabilities.

Useful exercises include the following: breath awareness, body scan, leaves-on-a-stream (defusion), and loving-kindness (compassion). These guided mindfulness exercises are freely available online.[2]

Strategy 2: Rehumanizing Learning

As higher education becomes increasingly marketized and commodified, learning has also become increasingly dehumanizing when the system socializes students to focus more on employability than their full range of aspirations, authenticity, and responsibilities toward their individual and collective flourishing (Kahn, 2017). To rehumanize learning, students are supported to go beyond the fear of failure or negative judgment to embrace their vulnerabilities and fully participate in critical reflection and dialogue.

Learning materials—Instead of privileging materials on technical competence, instructors may consider using materials that provoke new perspectives and compassion for self and others. In developing course syllabi, it is important to apply the strategy of "incremental" understanding (i.e., choosing a range of materials such as academic articles, videos, experiential activities, etc.) that progressively prepare the co-learners psychologically to discuss the so-called difficult topics of SJ-EDI and to strengthen their critical analytical capacity.

For example, in the first class of an urban health promotion course, the combined use of the video *The Danger of a Single Story* by Adichie (2009), an article on discussing "thorny" issues in class (Alexakos et al., 2016), and a postcolonial critique of the foundations of the Ottawa Charter of Health Promotion (McPhail-Bell, Fredericks, and Brough, 2013) worked effectively as a catalyst for critical awareness and reflection on power relations.

Many co-learners shared in the course evaluation that these required materials enabled them to realize that having assumptions is common to being human; what they appreciated was the opportunity to dialogue about the power embedded in these assumptions.

Resonant texts—Drawing on the essence embedded in the term "resonance," the first author (Wong) coined the term "resonant texts" as objects of expression created by research participants or co-learners to represent their perspectives, situational identities, lived experiences, and sense of being in the world, as well as their resonance to learning materials and group discussions (Wong, 2011; Wong et al., 2013). Co-learners may construct resonant texts using one or multiple mediums (e.g., painting, photos, collage, songs/lyrics, drawings, poems, stories, sculptures, etc.).

In the context of transformative learning, resonant texts can be used to replace conventional course assignments that privilege cognitive or technical knowing to encourage the co-learners to (re)connect to a full range of knowing—cognitive, emotive, embodied, social, and spiritual—which are co-constituted as they encounter their social worlds. Co-learners are invited to synthesize course materials, class discussions, and their own embodied resonance into resonant texts and present them to each other.

Wong's experience suggested that at the beginning, co-learners tended to feel hesitant and skeptical about creating resonant texts. They found it difficult to "deviate" from cognitive analysis and conventional ways of writing that often suppress or exclude the authors' authentic selves. However, their perspectives changed by mid-term, as captured in a quote from the course evaluation: "I am amazed at this authentic learning experience. It allowed us to connect to our inner self that is tied to who we are as nurses and in how we care for others."

Strategy 3: Embodied Integration of Value-Guided Experiential Learning

Learning is always embodied. Our knowing "depends on being in a world that is inseparable from our bodies, our language, and our social history" (Varela, Thompson, and Rosch, 1991, p. 149). Drawing on Merleau-Ponty's work on the lived body, Desmond and Jowitt (2012) suggest that embodied experiences do not "belong solely to the person" but are "constructed with others in the present" (p. 223). Thus, transformative learning is necessarily embodied. The authors have used a range of interactive learning activities that promote the integration of personal and collective values to promote commitment actions.

The Exclusionary Circle Game—This game begins with all participants being inside a circle. Each participant randomly receives one color-coded card, which represents a character with lived experiences associated with racism, patriarchy, homophobia, transphobia, and so on. Participants holding a marginalized status card are asked to leave the circle in sequence and go to designated spaces separated from others. Eventually, only one-half of the participants are left in the circle (see Wong and Li, 2015 for detailed instructions and application results). This learning activity has been used with undergraduate and graduate co-learners.

Debriefing engages co-learners in critical reflection and dialogue about structural violence and how their embodied responses are connected to their vulnerabilities and fundamental human values of empathy and fairness, as captured in a co-learner's reflection: "I wanted to stop it, but I was afraid. I can't believe this, even though it was a game, I felt vulnerable and did not want to draw any additional attention."

The Privilege Walk—This is an activity that supports co-learners to experientially connect with and make sense of their social positioning in a group setting. During the activity, the instructor reads out statements of privileges and marginalized statuses and invites co-learners to take a step forward or backward based on how their lived experiences are aligned with the statements. When all the statements have been read, co-learners are invited to note their social positioning relating to others in the group, and the instructor leads a debriefing session (see UBC Centre for Teaching, Learning and Technology, n.d. for detailed instructions).

Co-learners' responses during debriefing echoed Freire's (2000/1970) assertion that oppressions and social injustices dehumanize all people (i.e., both the privileged and marginalized individuals and communities). Many expressed their frustration about the persisting unequal power relations between Indigenous and non-Indigenous peoples and recognized their own responsibility in reducing social inequities through committed action.

The Neighborhood Exploration—This is an experiential activity developed as a group assignment. The purpose is to provide an opportunity for co-learners to work in small groups to integrate and apply everything that they have learned from the course materials to critical self-reflection, in-class dialogues, and new search of evidence on social and health equities into presentations on health equity and committed action. Each group visits and compares two neighborhoods that differ or contrast concerning socioeconomic, sociocultural, and sociopolitical characteristics.

Co-learners are to: focus on the privileges, vulnerabilities, and resilience of their chosen populations/communities; examine how intersecting social oppressions and systemic barriers impact the health and well-being of these populations/communities; engage in firsthand neighborhood observations and resonance; and draw on population health data, research evidence, media reports, and other relevant sources to identify the health disparities and potential effective community health-promotion strategies.

Groups are encouraged to engage in committed action to bring social change. Some examples of committed action undertaken by co-learners include the following: letters sent to local employers to advocate for reducing the stigma of mental illness at the workplace; petitions to provincial members of the government to advocate for affordable housing; and using social media to speak out against racism and other injustices.

Reflections from the co-learners illustrate the transformative potential of this activity, as one co-learner shares: "This assignment opened my eyes to disparities that I was not aware. What we read and see in the secondary data became real."

CONCLUSION

Integrating SJ-EDI in higher education is critical and needed now more than ever to counter the impact of neoliberalism in higher education and around the world. ACE is a rehumanizing approach that supports co-learners in their journey of awareness, discovery, acceptance, and transformation.

ACE processes (see Figure 9.1) are useful in guiding the development of learning activities that integrate reflective, embodied, and relational strategies to promote among the co-learners a critical understanding of interbeing, practices of compassion, and (re)connection to the fundamental human values of justice, equity, and collective well-being. These processes also contribute to their individual and collective resilience.

NOTES

1. ACT is an evidence-based third-wave psychological and behavior therapy that highlights the paradox of psychological problem solving (i.e., people's psychological pain worsens when they try to avoid it or get rid of it). ACT promotes awareness that the human mind constantly produces judgmental thoughts and support learners to find new ways of relating to these thoughts and feelings and move toward living fully through committed actions guided by chosen values.

2. Editorial note: Also, see Gill-Lopez chapter on implicit bias and mindfulness in Volume 2.

REFERENCES

Adichie, C. N. (2009). The danger of a single story (Video file). Retrieved April 1, 2018, from http://www.ted.com/talks/chimamanda_adichie_the_danger_of_a_single_story.

Alexakos, K., et al. (2016). Mindfulness and discussing "thorny" issues in the classroom. *Cultural Studies of Science Education, 11*(3), 741–69. doi:10.1007/s11422-015-9718-0.

Asher, N. (2003). Engaging difference: Towards a pedagogy of interring. *Teaching Education, 14*(3), 235–247. doi:10.1080/1047621032000135159

Desmond, B., and Jowitt, A. (2012). Stepping into the unknown dialogical experiential learning. *The Journal of Management Development, 31*(3), 221–30. doi:10.1108/02621711211208853.

Fernandes, L. (2003). *Transforming feminist practice: Non-violence, social justice and the possibilities of a spiritualized feminism.* San Francisco: Aunt Lute Books.

Freire, P. (2000/1970). *Pedagogy of the oppressed.* New York: Continuum.

Grigg, T., and Tidwell, D. (2015). Learning to teach mindfully: Examining the self in the context of multicultural education. *Teacher Education Quarterly, 42*(2), 87–104.

Harding, S. (Ed.). (2011). *The postcolonial science and technology studies reader.* Durham: Duke University Press.

Hayes, S. C., Strosahl, K., and Wilson, K. G. (1999). *Acceptance and commitment therapy: An experiential approach to behavior change*. New York: Guilford Press.
Heron, J. (1996). *Co-operative Inquiry. Research into the human condition*. London: Sage.
Hofmann, S. G., Sawyer, A. T., Witt, A. A., and Oh, D. (2010). The effect of mindfulness-based therapy on anxiety and depression: A meta-analytic review. *Journal of Consulting and Clinical Psychology*, 78(2), 169–83. doi:10.1037/a0018555.
hooks, b. (2000). *All about love: New vision*. New York: HarperCollins.
Kahn, P. E. (2017). The flourishing and dehumanization of students in higher education. *Journal of Critical Realism*, 16(4), 368–82. doi:10.1080/14767430.2017.1347444.
Kroth, M., and Cranton, P. (2014). *Stories of transformative learning*. Boston: Sense Publishers.
Li, A. T., Fung, K. P., Maticka-Tyndale, E., and Wong, J. P. (2017). Effects of HIV stigma reduction interventions in diasporic communities: Insights from the CHAMP Study. *AIDS Care,* 24:1–7. doi: 10.1080/09540121.2017.1391982.
Li, A. T., and Wong, J. P. (2016). CHAMP: Mobilizing people living with HIV and allies to champion HIV prevention and care in ethno-racial communities. *Prevention in Focus: Spotlights on Programming and Research, Fall 2016* (Published by CATIE). Available at: http://www.catie.ca/en/news/catie-exchange/2016-08-10.
Martinez-Cola, M., with English, R., Min, J., Peraza, J., Tambah, J., and Yebuah, C. (2018). When pedagogy is painful: Teaching in tumultuous times. *Teaching Sociology*, 46(2), 97–111. doi:10.1177/0092055X17754120.
McPhail-Bell, K., Fredericks, B., and Brough, M. (2013). Beyond the accolades: A postcolonial critique of the foundations of the Ottawa charter. *Global Health Promotion*, 20(2), 22.
Nhất Hạnh, T. (1987). *Interbeing: Fourteen Guidelines for Engaged Buddhism*. Berkeley, CA: Parallax.
Nhất Hạnh, T. (1997). *Teachings on love*. Boston: Shambhala Publications.
Nhất Hạnh, T. (2003). *Creating true peace: Ending violence in yourself, your family, your community, and the world*. New York: Free Press.
Singh, M., Manathunga, C., Bunda, T., and Jing, Q. (2016). Mobilising Indigenous and non-western theoretic-linguistic knowledge in doctoral education. *Knowledge Cultures*, 4(1), 56–70.
UBC Centre for Teaching, Learning and Technology. (n.d.). *User guide for educators. Theme II: Social Position—Privilege Walk*. Retrieved from http://timeandplace.ubc.ca/user-guide/theme-ii/privilege-walk-version-1/.
Varela, F., Thompson, E., and Rosch, E. (1991). *The embodied mind: Cognitive science and human experience*. Cambridge, MA: MIT Press.
Wang, C.-L. (2017). No-self, natural sustainability and education for sustainable development. *Educational Philosophy and Theory*, *49*(5), 550–561. doi: 10.1080/00131857.2016.1217189
Wong, J. P. (2011). *Being-Doing-Becoming Manly Men: A Bourdieusian exploration of the construction of masculine identities and sexual practices of young*

men (Doctoral Dissertation, University of Toronto). Ottawa: National Library of Canada. Available at: https://tspace.library.utoronto.ca/handle/1807/29913.

Wong, J. P. and Li, A. T. (2015) The exclusionary circle game: A tool to promote critical dialogue about HIV stigma and social justice. *Progress in Community Health Partnerships: Research, Education, and Action*, 91(3), 431–38.

Wong, J. P., Whalen, J., Abulencia, M. K., Abraham, V., Chandrashekhar, C., Ho, J., and Yeung, C. L. (August 2013). *Cultures, identities, and voices: An exploratory study on the sociocultural determinants of Asian young women's sexual health in Toronto*. Poster presentation at 21st IUHPE World Conference on Health Promotion, Pattaya, Thailand. doi:10.13140/RG.2.2.16599.52649.

Part V

REFLECTION FOR CRITICAL CONSCIOUSNESS

Chapter Ten

Tools for Raising a Critical Consciousness

Amy Bergstrom

Teaching for social justice across disciplines in higher education has a long history. Since Paulo Freire's groundbreaking work on critical pedagogy, educators have been incorporating ideas about equity into courses and curriculum. This chapter is based on several premises: (1) educators need to be culturally fluent to work with a changing demographic student population; (2) to achieve cultural fluency, critical reflection is necessary; and (3), teaching for social justice is rooted in critical pedagogy that requires developing a critical consciousness.

With these premises as a starting point, the chapter will describe how the Intercultural Development Inventory (IDI) is used as a pre- and post-tool to guide students through the process of self-reflection to develop a critical consciousness in preparation for social action. The students cultivate their awareness, knowledge, skills, and subsequently develop an action plan through the development and implementation of a capstone project based in part through their individual work with the IDI while actively engaged in equity, diversity, and inclusion (EDI) objectives through a series of four courses, which are delivered exclusively online.

The course sequence includes: "Developing Intercultural Competence," "Culturally Inclusive Learning Communities," "Universal Design for Learning and Critical Pedagogy," and "Teaching and Leading for Social Change." Hammer (2012) indicates that both online and face-to-face formats appear to help students develop their intercultural competence.

SELF-REFLECTION:
DEVELOPING A CRITICAL CONSCIOUSNESS

Varied processes of developing a critical consciousness are well-documented in the literature, and critical reflection is one of many. Larrivee (2000) describes the process of self-reflection as a cyclical process of examination, struggle, and perceptual shift. Challenging pre-service teachers to engage in self-reflection is a critical step in preparing them to teach for social justice. It is a powerful process to understand one's own biases and backgrounds, to develop a high degree of self-awareness (Rincón, 2009).

Social justice educators, regardless of their discipline, share a commitment to social change and uncovering unconscious bias that can lead to a deeper understanding of the world around them. Reflection can be difficult because it forces us to be honest with ourselves and identify areas needing improvement (Scales, 2008). However, self-reflection is necessary as the first step towards social justice action.

THE INTERCULTURAL DEVELOPMENT
INVENTORY AND CRITICAL REFLECTION

One tool to help students develop a critical consciousness orientation is the IDI. The IDI was developed by Bennett and Hammer (1998) to measure intercultural sensitivity objectively; it is a valid and reliable tool (Greenholtz, 2000). It can be used across disciplines to assess cultural sensitivity and competence (Hammer, 2012; Kruse, Didion, and Perzynski, 2014) and has been applied broadly in service-learning projects, mentorship programs, business settings, social work programs, and teacher education (Hammer, 2015).

The IDI is a fifty-item questionnaire that is administered electronically and measures intercultural development based on a continuum (Kruse, Didion, and Perzynski, 2014). The IDI was constructed to measure the orientation toward cultural differences as described in the Development Model of Intercultural Sensitivity (DMIS) (Hammer, Bennett, and Wiseman, 2003).

The IDI is a great tool to support critical reflection. Greenholtz (2000) writes that it is reflecting and re-reflecting on the significance of an experience or event that advances students' understanding about any subject. Mayhew (2007) asserts that opportunities for self-reflection provide students the ability to explore and examine assumptions and biases. Moreover, IDI research indicates that when students are given opportunities to reflect on their experiences and make meaning of those experiences, their intercultural competence further develops (Hammer, 2012).

The IDI is more than a measurement tool; more importantly, it provides guidelines on learning interventions that build intercultural competence (Hammer, 2015). It allows educators to assess the developmental readiness of their students to pursue various types of intercultural learning and to select and sequence learning activities that contribute to their development of intercultural competence (Bennett, Bennett, and Allen, 2003).

The results of the IDI provide a trained interpreter with an individual or group profile that can be translated into action plans for individuals, groups, or organizations (Greenholtz, 2000). To become a certified IDI interpreter, you must go through the IDI LLC company to get trained. The trained interpreter, in this case, is an adjunct faculty member who is a certified IDI interpreter. A small stipend is paid to the interpreter for their time meeting one-on-one with students. The trained interpreter meets one-on-one with students either via phone or using Zoom web conferencing.

Any faculty or staff member interested in EDI work can consider becoming a certified interpreter. It is also important to note, however, the interpreter does not have to be a part of your department or even your institution. The importance is that they are a trained certified interpreter, as only certified individuals can gain access to the tool and distribute the link so students can take the IDI.

The profile results and the development plan provide detailed guidance to further develop the student's intercultural competence (Hammer, 2012). One reason the IDI is so effective is that it not only measures how culturally competent people think they are but also how competent they actually are (Kruse, Didion, and Prezynski, 2014).

Taking the IDI and working with the results, which are arrayed along the Intercultural Development Continuum, is a powerful reflective exercise. These results range from the monocultural mind-set of Denial and Polarization, through the orientation of Minimization to Acceptance and Adaptation (Hammer, 2012).

The IDI is effective for faculty across the curricular spectrum to gain valuable information regarding individual student growth as well. Social justice educators must provide students with tools that will assist them in working toward equity and justice (Burrell Storms, 2012). The IDI is just such a tool. These intercultural assessment tools help educators to better understand and measure the effectiveness of their initiatives with students.

Finally, Ridley, Baker, and Hill (2001) ascertain that it is not enough to simply provide students opportunities to develop cultural competence but rather also to provide outcomes and steps necessary for action.

SOCIAL JUSTICE IN ACTION:
A GUIDED CURRICULAR PROCESS

Taking the IDI is the first step in utilizing this tool to further develop students' cultural competence and social justice action efforts. In the first course in the four-course sequence, students take the inventory. Once the instructor sends the course roster to the designated trained interpreter, the students receive a link to the questionnaire. It can be completed in one hour or less.

Upon completion, students receive an electronic copy of their results, which prepares them to meet one-on-one with the interpreter to go over their results. The IDI generates an individual profile report and a customized Intercultural Development Plan (IDP or Plan). Students may use this plan as a roadmap on their journey toward increasing cultural competence and, ultimately, developing a critical consciousness. The students decide whether or not to share their detailed results with their faculty member.

When students meet with the trained interpreter, awareness, knowledge, and skills are discussed, which helps them make sense of their results. This debriefing process is required and an essential part of the process, once students' beliefs, values, or worldview have been challenged (Hartwell et al., 2017)

The intended outcome of the plan is a customized profile, revealing for the student where gaps exist and areas for growth (Hermanson, 2018). To acquire knowledge, develop skills, and engage in action, students must first develop an awareness of their own social and cultural identities, values, and biases (Hartwell et al., 2017). The IDI does this.

Once the students have taken the IDI, received their results, and met with the trained interpreter, they are ready to develop both short- and long-term goals that address the results. Goal setting is important as it draws from all EDI components as well as feeling manageable to students (Burrell Storms, 2012).

The goal-setting process is the first step in moving students toward action. For example, a short-term goal might be to attend a community cultural event with a diverse group, or another student might choose to read a selection of books representing a cultural or religious perspective different than their own. Students share these experiences with one another in class and develop written reflections.

Once the goals are established, students begin to work toward meeting their goals. Progress indicators are used to assess progress on goals. These progress assessments are where students identify what goals have been met or unmet and further refine their plan. Identifying barriers to meeting these goals is also established so students develop a strategy to address the barriers. The reflection and self-assessing are done as an ongoing assignment throughout the four-course sequence. Students are engaged in course readings on goal setting and current research around social justice education.

The goal-setting process also is important as it helps students to develop the skills necessary to develop and implement their social justice action project. The social justice action project is the culmination of students' work over a period of time. The social justice action project is important, as Burrell Storms (2012) writes that social justice educators must provide students with opportunities to engage in a social action project.

The students' goals are reinforced and revisited throughout the course sequence. The specific pedagogies delivered over the course sequence support EDI objectives and are scaffolded throughout the courses. For example, journaling provides students an opportunity to examine bias and assumptions and question long-held beliefs in a safe space. The journals are private between the student and the faculty member.

Scales (2008) identifies writing as an effective way to make sense of experiences, specifically to organize thinking and assess and learn from the experience. Writing cultivates awareness and develops habits of critical reflection. Students journal on the progress made on their goals.

Another effective strategy used with education students, for example, is through the use of case studies. Students read and analyze case studies that build communication skills, analyze for bias, and apply and develop suggestions for solutions that can be applied to their own classrooms. Case studies offer students opportunities to examine situations from multiple vantage points. Gorski and Pothini (2014) believe case studies require more critical reflection and challenge students to ask deeper questions.

Finally, the students retake the IDI in the fourth and final course. The purpose of retaking the IDI is to measure growth over time after the students have been exposed to various teaching and learning modalities around EDI. Specific activities that occur between the first taking of the IDI and second include the following: journals, critical analysis of readings, discussion board posts, case studies, short videos, synchronous class meetings, and attending, participating, and interacting in cross-cultural community events.

Connections made outside of class are essential to developing social justice educators. It is one thing to engage with classmates, but providing students opportunities and ensuring they have the skills to be successful in navigating difference and discomfort is essential. Fuentes, Chanthongthip, and Rios (2010) write that one way to connect students with social justice is to have them make personal connections. This can only happen when students engage with communities and participate in events that are new, different, and outside of their scope of habits. This is the action.

Once students have taken the IDI a second time, they are ready to finalize their social justice projects. The projects stem from their IDI results and goals. Some example projects include the following: community book clubs around EDI, increasing the visibility of homelessness through school and community meetings, developing a multicultural student union to combat racism, and advocacy training for community members around social justice issues.

Each project is developed through careful teaching around the tenets of the EDI framework (i.e., awareness, knowledge, skills, and action), which is shared in the Hartwell et al. (2017) chapter, and each student's IDI results.

Opportunities to reflect, interact, and engage with content that is challenging happens over time. Medina-López-Portillo (2004) cites the longer a program is, the more developed one's intercultural competence becomes, as the IDI can measure change over time. Fuentes, Chanthongthip, and Rios (2010) describe the limitations of relying on one course toward the teaching and learning of social justice. It is for this reason we spread this important work out over the sequence of four courses.

CONCLUSION

Mayhew (2007) writes that at the heart of higher education institutions' mission is the responsibility to graduate students with the capacity and skills to be thoughtful and responsible citizens in a diverse democratic society. Teaching for social justice in the context of EDI across disciplines works toward achieving the mission of higher education.

This chapter describes the process of achieving the goals and outcomes of EDI, through a guided process, primarily using the IDI. Learning occurs when we expose our students to new ways of thinking about themselves and the world around them (Mayhew, 2007). Developing critical thinkers and teaching for social justice can create, in part, a more just society.

REFERENCES

Bell, L., and Griffin, P. (2007). Designing social justice education courses. In M. Adams, L. A. Bell, and P. Griffin (Eds.) (2nd ed.). *Teaching for Diversity and Social Justice* (pp. 67–87). New York: Routledge.

Bennett, M. J., and Hammer, M. R. (1998, 2001). *The Intercultural Development Inventory (IDI): Manual*. Portland: The Intercultural Communication Institute.

Bennett, J. M., Bennett, M. J., and Allen, W. (2003). Developing intercultural competence in the language classroom. In D. L. Lange and R. M. Paige (Eds.), *Culture as the core: Perspectives on culture in second language learning.* Greenwich, CT: Information Age Publishing.

Burrell Storms, S. (2012). Preparing students for social action in a social justice education course: What works? *Equity and Excellence in Education*, 45(4), 547–60.

Fuentes, R., Chanthongthip, L., and Rios, F. (2010). Teaching and learning social justice as an intellectual community requirement: Pedagogical opportunities and student understandings. *Equity and Excellence in Education*, 43(3), 357–74.

Gay, G., and Kirkland, K. (2003). Developing cultural critical consciousness and self-reflection in pre-service teacher education. *Theory into Practice*, 42(3), 181–87.

Gorski, P., and Pothini, S. (2014). *Case studies on diversity and social justice education.* New York: Routledge.

Grant C., and Sleeter, C. (2010). Race, class, gender, and disability in the classroom. In J. Banks and C. Banks (Eds.), *Multicultural education: Issues and perspective* (7th ed.) (pp. 233–56). Hoboken, NJ: Wiley.

Greenholtz, J. (2000). Assessing cross-cultural competence in transnational education: The Intercultural development Inventory. *Higher Education in Europe*, 25(3), 411–16.

Hammer, M. (2015). *Why should you consider using the Intercultural Development Inventory?* Retrieved from http://idiinventory.com.

Hammer, M. (2012). The Intercultural Development Inventory: A new frontier in assessment and development of intercultural competence. In M. Van de Berg, R. M. Paige, and K. Hemming Lou (Eds.) (pp. 115–35). *Student learning abroad: What our students are learning, what they are not, and what we can do about it.* Sterling, VA: Stylus Publishing.

Hammer, M., Bennett, M., and Wiseman, R. (2003). Measuring intercultural sensitivity: the Intercultural Development Inventory. *International Journal of Intercultural Relations.* 27, 421–43.

Hartwell, E., Cole, K., Donovan, S., Greene, R., Burrell Storms, S., and Williams, T. (2017). Breaking down silos: Teaching for equity, diversity, and inclusion across disciplines. *Humboldt Journal of Social Relations* 1(39): 143–62.

Hermanson, D. (2018). Using IDI guided development to increase intercultural competence. *Culminating Projects in Education Administration and Leadership.* 41. Retrieved from http://repository.st.cloudstate.edu/edad_etds/41.

Kruse, J., Didion, J., and Perzynski, K. (2014). Utilizing the Intercultural Development Inventory to develop intercultural competence. *Springerplus*, 3, 334.

Lantz-Deaton, C. (2017). Internationalizations and the development of students' intercultural competence. *Teaching in Higher Education*, 22(5), 532–50.

Larrivee, B. (2000). Transforming teaching practice: Becoming the critically reflective teacher. *Reflective Practice*, 1(3), 293–307.

Mayhew, M. J. (2007). Pedagogical practices that contribute to social justice outcomes. *Review of Higher Education*, 31(1), 55–80.

Medina-López-Portilio, A. (2004). Intercultural learning assessment: The link between program duration and the development of intercultural sensitivity. *The Interdisciplinary Journal of Study Abroad*, 10, 179–99.

National Education Association (2008). *Promoting educators' cultural competence to better serve culturally diverse students, A policy brief.* Retrieved from https://www.nea.org/assets/docs/PB13_CulturalCompetence08.pdf.

Pratt-Johnson, Y. (2006). Communicating cross-culturally: What teachers should know. *The Internet TESL Journal*, 12(2). Retrieved from http://iteslj.org/.

Ridley, C., Baker, D., and Hill, C. (2001). Critical issues concerning cultural competence. *The Counseling Psychologist*, 29(6), 790–821.

Rincón, A. (2009). Practicing cultural humility. In T. Berthold, J. Miller, and A. Avila-Esparza (Eds.), *Foundations for Community Health Workers* (pp. 136–54). San Francisco: Jossey-Bass.

Scales, P. (2008). *Teaching in the lifelong learning sector*. London: Open University Press. Retrieved from https://www.amazon.ca/Teaching-Lifelong-Learning-Sector-Scales/dp/0335222404ISBN.

Chapter Eleven

A Person-Centered Approach to Facilitate Students' Social Advocacy

Stephaney Morrison

This chapter presents a person-centered approach to a graduate social justice counseling class that embraces transformational pedagogy and learning while fostering a community of trust. After an introduction to the person-centered approach and its roots in social justice education and advocacy, the chapter examines five different goals that make up the approach, along with sample assignments and activities and their connection to EDI. While the assignments are from a counselor education course, they have broad applicability across disciplines and can be used in an undergraduate laboratory or seminar-type setting.

Person-centered teaching and learning are defined as the type of teaching that protects and promotes students' innate creative capacities of learning from their experiences and to promote wholeness and integration in the individual by focusing on their personal growth, creativity, and development into competent members of society.

This approach is a nonauthoritative approach, where the instructor shares authority with students, leading students to participate in the process of learning and discovering their own voice. The instructor's role is that of a facilitator who listens without judgment and acknowledges the students' experience without interfering with the process of self-discovery (Zucconi, 2015; Quin, 2012).

Therefore, in the school counseling course, students participate with each other in a community of learners in which they examine their cultural identities and reflect on their roles and engagement in social justice advocacy work with the K-12 population. While students are developing content knowledge in the course, the person-centered pedagogical strategy is used to give students space to deepen their sense of social justice as change agents.

Further, this approach guides students as they identify personal biases and oppressive policies that impede equitable access for the students and families they serve in the education system. Finally, the person-centered approach works especially well with the social justice paradigm that informs counselor education training because of the emphasis on respecting the life and dignity of all individuals. Educators in other disciplines might have similar paradigms guiding their training.

Although a singular conceptualization of social justice has been a daunting task, social welfare and human dignity of individuals emerge as essential to it. Scholars from various disciplines maintain that social justice must start with unveiling oppression (Decker, Manis, and Paylo, 2015). Historically, marginalized individuals and groups have been indoctrinated with the hegemonic beliefs and values of dominant groups (e.g., white, male, middle-class, etc.) (Crethar, Rivera, and Nash, 2008). Social justice starts with raising the consciousness, or the veil, of the oppressed.

Further, scholars argue that individuals who serve the oppressed must be aware of their attitudes and behaviors that perpetuate the oppression of their clients and work on a systemic level to provide services for their clients (Hays and Erford, 2018). In addition, for social advocacy to be an important part of counselor education training, or training in other disciplines, there needs to be a shift in graduate school training.

Lee (2014) argued that if counselors are to be agents of change, then they must move beyond the traditional roles and scope of counseling to identify the relationship between injustices (i.e., oppression, discrimination, and prejudice) and the mental health of marginalized groups in order to provide equitable access of services.

Lee (2007) proposed five personal action steps: (1) exploring your personal life's meaning and commitment, (2) exploring personal privilege, (3) exploring the nature of oppression, (4) working to become multicultural literate, and (5) establishing a personal social justice compass.

School counselors with a social justice orientation focus on these principles collectively in a school counseling course in an effort to address injustices faced by disenfranchised K-12 students and families. These are also applicable to all genre and discipline.

Some scholars have noted that despite the increased attention given to social justice counseling and increasing awareness of students, trainees/students report feeling unprepared to engage in advocacy and do not participate in this type of work to a large extent (Bemak and Chung, 2011; Edwards et al., 2017).

To bridge this gap in the training of school counseling students for social action and potentially students in other fields who work with diverse populations, the person-centered teaching and learning goals, adapted from Barret-Lennard (1998, pp. 187–88), create the conditions (e.g., empathy, respect, and congruence) necessary to provide psychological safety in the classroom. This offers students an environment that encourages reflection and awareness about personal biases that are harmful to clients.

THE PERSON-CENTERED TEACHING AND LEARNING GOALS

Central to the person-centered approach are five goals. Goal one is to create a climate of trust in which curiosity and natural desire to learn can be nourished and enhanced. Building a climate of trust is essential in counseling to facilitate growth, and it is foundational to effective classroom learning across disciplines. Many counseling students come to class with significant anxieties and fears about social justice and advocacy issues. Therefore, it is necessary to facilitate trust and safety in the classroom for students so as to encourage self-reflection and group reflection as necessary in this process.

One way in which this is realized in this classroom setting is through group-building activities. These activities help students to connect, to feel capable, and have opportunities provided to contribute to the greater needs of the group.

One activity that can be used across disciplines is an immersion or experiential assignment. Students are challenged to consider a particular marginalized group about which they have preconceived notions. This process is done in small groups in class a few weeks into the semester when trust has been developed among their peers. The students are asked to reflect on what preconceived notions they have about the group(s) and to consider the basis of these preconceptions. After students identify the marginalized population and process their feelings within a safe space with their peers, they are encouraged to share in a large group.

The next part of the assignment is for students to visit the identified community at least four times. In one of the visits, students must interview a member of that community. Students are expected to journal about their feelings and the details of what happened while they were there.

The final part of the assignment is that students create a social justice advocacy plan for that group based on what they learned as an observer and researcher and meet in small groups to process their experience. This activity builds community and challenges the preconceptions, assumptions, and biases of students. They can do this kind of work within a safe space while also seeing that there are other people who struggle with assumptions. Students have reflected that this is a powerful assignment for them.

Goal two is promoting a participatory mode in all aspects of learning and decision making to further self-responsibility. In this person-centered learning goal, students are empowered to learn that they are integral to the learning and teaching process. They must contribute to the class's reservoir of knowledge. The goal is for them to internalize the value, for their future practice, of flattening the hierarchy and promoting equity, diversity, and inclusion (EDI).

For a sample assignment, each student in the school counseling class is assigned a topic for each week of the semester (i.e., chapter in the main text, articles, etc.). They are included in facilitating the class for that session. The students are encouraged to present the material using personal style of presentation and focusing on important aspects of the lesson that are applicable to their role as school counselors. Not only does this build their facultative role as a school counselor, but they are also connecting as peers.

Further, students are encouraged to identify an issue that school counselors are struggling with district-, state-, or nation-wide and to lead the class into discussion. Some topics that were highly effective and meaningful for them were issues such as school violence, grief and loss, homelessness, and the school-prison pipeline. At the end of the semester, each student has participated as a co-repertory of knowledge. They now understand, through experience, the value of including students in the teaching and learning process.

In addition to supporting EDI goals, this approach promotes active learning that focuses more on developing students' skills than on transmitting information. This requires that students engage in higher-order thinking. In their seminal work, Bonwell and Eison defined strategies that promote active learning as "instructional activities involving students in doing things and thinking about what they are doing" (1991). This helps students to explore their own attitudes and values and confront forms of injustice as they reflect and wrestle with the social justice topics.

Goal three builds on the previous two goals to increase students' capabilities to make personal meaning out of course content and understand the complexity of their present behavior and how they might behave in the future. Within this framework, students develop into critically reflective practitioners who are not just relying on the instructor for knowledge but are fully participating in generating knowledge through reflection.

Students are usually anxious and are not sure how much they are allowed to explore and experience meaning from the content. In goals one and two, the instructor facilitates and encourages students to share their earlier experiences, knowledge, and thinking to contribute to collective meaning-making in the classroom. In goal three, this practice of self-reflection is deepened to allow students both personal and collective space to reflect on EDI.

A general example of an assignment is the use of reflective videos on current social justice issues in the media that pertain to the topic of a given class. In one specific assignment, the topic is black and white students' differing perceptions of racial issues, such as police profiling. Students are asked to watch a video about the topic and jot down their observations and feelings. The students are then encouraged to process their reflections with one or two peers. They then come back to the larger group and are encouraged to share their experiences and reflect on the connection to social justice advocacy in K-12 education.

This type of activity takes the spotlight off the instructor as the sole bearer of authority and knowledge. It teaches students how to be learners within a community that is committed to building a repository of knowledge upon which everyone in the class can draw.

Goal four involves helping students to achieve results they appreciate and consider worthwhile and inwardly meaningful by confronting their resistances. Students come with varied backgrounds and experiences to the classroom. In this environment, resistances and subtle hostilities can abound.

Nonverbal resistance can take the form of silence and is evidenced by students doodling and/or playing with their phones. Resistance can also be in the form of microaggressions. For students to gain results that are worthwhile to them, proper facilitation of discussion is important.

Any topic on social justice issues, especially as it relates to race, can incite strong emotions. While potentially uncomfortable, this can also propel social change and transformation. Of course, pedagogical approaches should suit the teacher's beliefs about the utility of the expression of emotions (Buckley and Foldy, 2010; Hays and Erford, 2018).

As students are challenged while reflecting on the feelings they experience, students are developing important skills/competencies as future school counselors or practitioners in a wide variety of fields. In fact, they are creating within themselves core conditions significant to creating a safe place for their future clients.

These core conditions are authenticity/genuineness, empathic understanding, and unconditional positive regard or respect. Person-centered scholars argue that as students develop these three conditions, they are in a pivotal position to develop pertinent critical-thinking skills and ethical consciousness (Buhin and Vera, 2009). In fact, students are challenged to develop moral courage to understand the current landscape of education and how to use social justice evidenced-based practices to provide equitable services for K-12 students and family.

A sample activity that helps students confront their resistances is a weekly reflective journal in which students log their reactions to the reading, current events, and social justice conversations outside of class with families and friends. Students also use this activity to ask questions they are not comfortable asking in a group discussion and to reflect on activities in the class that were impactful for them or not helpful.

The instructor uses this medium to give individualized feedback to students. This also gives the facilitator insights about how the students are journeying through the process of becoming culturally competent and socially active counselors, and a personal space in which to interact with the students. This reflective paper is also used as a conversation starter at the beginning of the class session each week.

Goal five involves encouraging instructors to grow personally by finding rich satisfaction in their interactions with learners and thus increasing their personal resourcefulness. For example, when preconceived biases are revealed, a faculty member of color can struggle to process such feelings. However, as an instructor builds trust within this community of learners, the instructor is encouraged to process with students as appropriate and significant to learning.

To that end, the content, the process, or the expectations of the course are not based on feelings but with the purpose of the course in mind. With a person-centered approach, students are encouraged to take risks and grow, despite experiencing discomfort and the resistance that accompanies it.

For example, one student struggling with the social justice aspect of the course stated that reflecting and processing one's biases and assumptions were not relevant to the type of work she will do as a school counselor. The student expected the instructor to proceed to the skills portion of the course, which she thought would benefit her more.

In this situation, the instructor met with the student to discuss the student's feelings and revisited the course goals. In addition, they discussed the goals and objectives that detail why the social justice focus of the class was important to school counselor training. For the rest of the semester, the instructor checked in with the student to assess her belief system and growth.

This approach was effective and gave the student an opportunity to not only identify her biases but to appreciate the learning goals of the course as part of her training. Additionally, it gave the student a safe space to honestly deal with her struggles and conflicts about social justice work and advocacy with diverse populations.

The student is not the only one who grows through this process. The facilitator is also learning as she challenges the thoughts of the students that are not responsive to the social justice goals of the class. The person-centered approach helps the instructor learn to challenge within the ethos of empathy, authenticity, and respect. Her goal is to remain nonjudgmental so that she can create an empathetic connection with her students.

CONCLUSION

The person-centered teaching and learning approach is student-centered, which connects faculty and students professionally in both undergraduate laboratory- seminar-type setting and graduate programs. It is a commitment to effective and democratic learning with the capacity to share passion about learning.

In this shared commitment, both instructor and students relate with respect, empathy, and congruence. The instructor is capable of being in touch with self, as well as the facilitator of learning that promote students' creativity and autonomy to explore stereotypes and prejudices that impact marginalized students and families. The students' role in this learning experience is to take responsibility for their own cultural development, and grow out of being uncomfortable.

REFERENCES

Barkley, E. (2010). *Student engagement techniques: A handbook for college faculty.* San Francisco: Jossey-Bass.

Barrett-Lennard, G. T. (1998). *Carl Rogers' helping system, journey and substance.* London: Sage.

Bemak, F., and Chung, R. (2011). Applications in social justice counselor training: Classroom without walls. *The Journal of Humanistic Counseling*, 50, 204–19.

Bonwell, C. C., and Eison, J. A. (1991). *Active learning: creating excitement in the classroom.* ASH#-ERIC Higher Education Report No. 1, Washington, DC: The George Washington University, School of Education and Human Development.

Buckley, T., and Foldy, E. G. (2010). A pedagogical model for increasing race-related multicultural counseling competency. *The Counseling Psychologists*, 38(5), 691–713. doi:10.1177/0011000009360917.

Buhin, L., and Vera, E. M. (2009). Preventing racism and promoting social justice: Person-centered and environment-centered interventions. *The Journal of Primary Prevention,* 30(1), 43–59. doi:10.1007/s10935-008-0161-9.

Crethar, H., Torres Rivera, E., and Nash, S. (2008). In search of common threads: Linking multicultural, feminist, and social justice counseling paradigms. *Journal of Counseling & Development, 86*, 269–278.

Decker, K. M., Manis, A. A., and Paylo, M. J. (2015). Infusing social justice advocacy into counselor education: Strategies and recommendations. *The Journal of Counselor Preparation and Supervision*, 8(3). Retrieved from http://dx.doi .org/10.7729/83.1092.

Edwards, L., Tate, K. A, Cook, J., Toigo, M., and Yeomans, A. (2017). Counselors as advocates: effects of a pilot project designed to develop advocacy knowledge and confidence in trainees. *Journal for Social Action in Counseling and Psychology*, 9(2), 79–93.

Hays D., and Erford, B. (2018). *Developing multicultural counseling competence: a systemic approach* (3rd ed.). New York: Pearson.

Lee, C. (2007). *Counseling for social justice* (2nd ed.). Alexandria, VA: American Counseling Association.

Lee, J. (2014). Asian international students' barriers to joining group counseling. *International Journal of Group Counseling*, 64, 445–64. doi:10.1521/ijgp.2014 .64.4.444.

Quin, A. (2012). A person-centered approach to multicultural counseling competence. *Journal of Humanistic Psychology*, 20(10), 1–50. doi:10.1177/0022167812458452.

Zucconi, A. (2015). Person-centered education. *Promoting leadership in thought that leads to action* 2(5).

Part VI

SAFE SPACES AND RESISTANCE

Chapter Twelve

Anticipating Resistances and Leveraging a Response

Kim Barber

In workshops or other educational settings such as the college classroom, discussions about equity, diversity, and inclusion (EDI) can ignite conflict, offense, and resistance. However, they can also engender understanding, healing, and progress. How can educators address topics related to EDI to gain productive discourse with students in higher education when many students, as well as faculty, experience intimidation and conflict around these discussions?

This chapter will demonstrate strategies to set the stage for open dialogue by anticipating resistance and talking about how to leverage conflict in order for students to gain understanding and healing through equity, diversity, and inclusion in a safe space.

While boundaries and ground rules are vital to the success of creating a safe space for productive discourse, it is equally important to anticipate typical resistances that you will encounter and to think about how you will respond to them. This chapter examines the four typical resistances of: (1) discomfort with talking organically and transparently, (2) students not understanding other cultural identity conflicts, (3) triggers, and (4) fear of not being understood.

After explaining and providing an example of each resistance, this chapter draws on the work of Kevin Kahakula'akea John Fong to discuss boundaries and ground rules that respond to the resistances. Fong is the founder and principal of Elemental Partners in California and is an expert in managing and setting effective boundaries for complex, controversial, and productive discourse. Fong's boundaries are, respective to each resistance, (1) "Respect the Space," (2) "Respect the Process," (3) "Respect Each Other," and (4) "Respect Yourself" (2018).

RESISTANCE ONE

Students may feel uncomfortable to talk organically and transparently. Once the topic of race or equality or inclusion is introduced, there is a knee-jerk reaction of discomfort. The brain signals negative thoughts and un-conscious biases; therefore, students become apprehensive about speaking organically and about truly exposing vulnerabilities. Goleman (2013) dis-covered that social pain is hardwired in the brain in a much more complex structure than physical. Therefore, our minds constantly re-create and reflect on it.

A sample story from a workshop that included students from different nationalities, one of whom had German heritage, demonstrates this. The student of German heritage approached the workshop facilitator to indicate that he was uncomfortable sharing with the larger group that he had German heritage. When the facilitator asked why, the student said that it was because there was a Turkish student in the workshop, and because of a history of war and conflict between Turkey and Germany, the German student was raised to be cautious around people of Turkish descent.

Respect the Space

How does a facilitator respond to the student of German heritage who was apprehensive about speaking of their culture? How can a facilitator address a learned suspicion of someone different? One effective response is to talk to the student about respecting the space. Respecting the space involves the understanding of knowing that it is a safe space for everyone.

Therefore, everyone should feel comfortable in the space knowing that each student will always have a sense of belonging and the confidence to feel valued because of the space. You may say something like, "Honor Con-fidentiality. Everyone in the space should sense belonging." Honor the space, and keep everything discussed in the room. This is one way to overcome resistance one.

Additionally, the student with the German heritage could directly share his feeling about fear and anxiety of why he does not want to share his heritage. Then the faculty could recharge by reminding students of how much courage it took to share. Afterward, the faculty could ask the students to assist them to feel comfortable in the space. If the student of German heritage still did not feel comfortable to share his fear and anxiety, then the faculty could share her heritage and how the faculty might feel if there was someone there from another heritage with whom there existed historical conflict.

Hopefully, this vulnerability would encourage the student with the German heritage to feel more comfortable to share. Reminding students of this in the beginning and reminding and encouraging throughout the class is critical.

RESISTANCE TWO

Students do not understand other cultural identities. Most students are more experienced with their own culture than others, and many students will have a limited knowledge and understanding of other people's cultures. Hence, this makes it challenging to identify when conflicts are rooted in cultural differences, as well as what to do about them.

For example, students in a white privilege workshop viewed a video of a project that showed a white millennial female from the South who commented that she did not understand why her African American friend kept talking about racism. The white woman in the video did not see the racism, so she thought her African American friend must be exaggerating or being oversensitive.

The reaction among the students in the white privilege workshop varied greatly. Some African American students were offended and confused that the white student in the video did not understand their marginalized history. Some white students said that they understood the reaction of the white student in the video. However, some white students in the workshop also felt that the white woman in the video was insensitive.

Respect the Process

Resistance two can be explained by the lack of understanding between cultural identities. Since most students are experts of their own culture, they look through the lens with one perspective. The white millennial female from the South in the video who commented about her lack of understanding of racism against African Americans demonstrated a one-way cultural perspective. The video had the desired effect of creating a dialogue between the students in the workshop about what we know about other people's perspectives from within their own culture.

The second boundary, "Respect the Process," is impactful in this situation. The facilitator can assess the situation as the students react to the video and then remind the students to "Be present and engaged, bring your best self: mind, heart, body and spirit" (Fong, 2018). The facilitator can emphasize that learning about different cultures and the conflict between cultures starts with honoring each other by being fully engaged.

This honor and engagement is part of the process and part of the journey to healing and feeling comfortable to speak more organically. The facilitator can honor the reaction of offense and confusion from the African American students but then suggest that the group also take time to try to understand (not excuse) the basis for the white student's comments. While the white student in the video was clearly incorrect in her understanding, the goal should be to understand where her incorrect view originated to discuss how to respond to a person with incorrect views so as to make this a learning moment. The facilitator can then emphasize that this is a great time to ask questions and not make judgments—though this can be very challenging.

Additionally, a workshop or discussion facilitator can use what the author describes as the "Middle Road Theory" to address Resistance Two. The Middle Road Theory is understanding that every perspective is that person's current reality. However, to get to a shared-reality that is not just that person's worldview is called the Middle Road Theory, which is where healing begins. The facilitator should encourage each participant to understand and try to visualize where the other person's perspective lives.

The goal of the Middle Road Theory is to understand, feel, and relate to the other's experience. The facilitator must emphasize that healing won't start until someone begins. The facilitator needs to encourage both sides to understand that the experience is still true and hurtful, even if you personally did not inflict the hurt.

RESISTANCE THREE

Students are subject to triggers from their own experiences. These discourses are very sensitive, and as Goleman (2013) has pointed out, students' negative experiences follow them more than positive experiences. Therefore, there is a high percentage of a chance that someone will be triggered through the conversations.

Here is a sample situation from a workshop on EDI. The facilitator asked the students to discuss how some employment systems in America have racial residues. A Latino student in the workshop talked about the experience of being hired for one job without being seen and then coming in and being told they did not have any openings. The student expressed that it made them feel inadequate and worthless. During this same discourse, another student recalled an experience where they felt worthless and were not able to get a job for which they knew they were qualified.

However, in this student's case, not only did they not get the job, but they were also told that they should just apply for something they are better suited for, such as cleaning. This second student was so upset that she then had to excuse herself from the workshop momentarily.

Respect Each Other

Resistance three, triggers from experiences, is a critical resistance. Triggers can be damaging to students experiencing them. Therefore, it is imperative to make this third boundary of Respecting Each Other a foundational rule for everyone to remember. This rule includes proclaiming the following: "All viewpoints and voices are valid. One person speaks at a time. Be in a place of nonjudgment and generous spirit." Ask students to be considerate of each other's experience and feelings. Allow students to journey through to get to healing if they are ready.

If not, allow the students to know they are safe and supported no matter whether the other students agree or not. It is fundamental for all students to know they are in a space where they are in control of how far they are ready to proceed. This particular section will be used to redirect or recharge the atmosphere many times to keep the space safe and comfortable.

In this scenario, there were students who were triggered by another student's feelings of inadequacy and devaluation. Though this may not seem like a big issue, we cannot assume we understand the wounds and fears of what a student experiences. In a case such as this, the facilitator might leave the room with a student who feels triggered and ask if the student is ready to talk or needs time. This would allow the student to feel supported in their feelings and emphasizes to the students that the facilitator understands.

The facilitator should also consider referring students for more emotional support. For example, refer students to your institution's Counseling Center or some other professional counseling department or center. This is a reminder that recharging is once again necessary to continue to keep students engaged and to remember the courage it takes to be vulnerable. Remember recharging the atmosphere is redirecting.

One technique that may also be used to address this situation is part of setting the atmosphere with boundaries and ground rules by allowing students to know it is a sensitive topic, and when they begin to experience a trigger, they should feel free to leave the room but to give a thumbs-up if they just need a moment and are OK. Or, if they are not, no thumbs-up will allow faculty to know to send staff or other faculty members to check on the student. Remember, faculty do not need to tackle this type of discourse on their own, but they can solicit assistance from other staff, such as campus counseling partners or other faculty.

RESISTANCE FOUR

Students fear not being understood. There are many students who do not identify with cultures other than their own. These students may experience anxiety and fear about discussing their experiences. This may lead to students feeling misunderstood.

In an example in which the workshop was discussing violence as a result of racism and prejudice, one female African American shared how she was sexually and brutally assaulted by a white male after-hours while leaving a night class. She started to cry. Some students were empathetic, but others were judgmental, asking "What did you do?" and "What were you wearing?" The female African American immediately shut down and did not share anymore about the situation. The faculty asked the student to step out with her while her colleagues rerouted the students back to boundaries and ground rules. The student shared with the faculty that she was afraid she would be misunderstood by sharing.

Respect Yourself

The fourth and final resistance is fear of not being understood. This can actually be experiencing the "real" fear of a situation. There are many situations where the vulnerabilities of students may cause fear. Many students, as we discussed in this resistance, could feel misunderstood if they do share, and therefore, they do not. In this scenario, the African American student experienced humiliation and real fear after she felt she was judged harshly after sharing her vulnerability.

The fourth boundary section, Respect Yourself, could include a rule such as, "Listen, speak, and act respectfully. Speak from your own perspective. Use 'I' statements." This is critical. Students must use "I" statements to keep a nonjudgmental environment and attitude. It also will keep generalizations to a minimum. It would be useful in this situation to remind the students to speak in phrases such as "I feel . . . because . . ." Faculty could then ask the African American student how that makes her feel and why. Then the atmosphere could be recharged with the comments to show respect for each other.

In this situation, the workshop facilitator applauded the African American student's bravery for her willingness to share. Then the facilitator stepped out of the space with the student so that the student could express herself freely. Finally, if there are other facilitators in the workshop, they can redirect students to use the "I" perspective and remind them all to respect each other by listening attentively and objectively. As students speak with the "I" statement, it is a reflection of respect, through speech and actions, toward each other as well as themselves. This also allows students to understand that it is only that student's opinion and does not invalidate their experience or feelings.

In this scenario, after returning to the classroom, the African American student found out that the recharge of respecting each other and themselves led to some of the students who had empathy toward her addressing the students who did not. This gave clarity and support for the African American student. Additionally, after the class, the other students who did not show empathy expressed to the workshop facilitator that they were insensitive but had grown up with the understanding that women, in general, were revered in a certain image. We then had a more detailed conversation about their beliefs. Later, the workshop facilitator discovered that the students did approach the African American young lady with remorse.

However, further conversations were necessary with these students to gain a better understanding of gender equality and respect. Therefore, though the boundaries are limited to the classroom, you may find that more healing and discourse is necessary. Much of the work with EDI is not a one-time solution but a life-long learning commitment and process.

CONCLUSION

Though topics related to EDI are sensitive, stimulating, and challenging, they simultaneously invoke change, awareness, healing, and can be a learning experience for all, including the workshop facilitator or faculty member. The purpose of this chapter was to demonstrate strategies to set the stage for a successful conversation by anticipating resistance and to leveraging conflict in order for students to gain understanding and healing about equity, diversity, and inclusion. Though students and faculty may experience intimidation and conflict, it is these very same resistances that may be used to promote healing, awareness, and education.

REFERENCES

Fong, K. J. (2018). *Proceedings from New Leadership Academy mid-year retreat.* Ann Arbor, MI.
Goleman, D. (2013). *Focus: The hidden driver of excellence.* New York: HarperCollins Publishers.

Chapter Thirteen

Curricular "Safe Spaces": Clarifying Potential Misconceptions

Chris Adamo

Recently, the notion of curricular "safe spaces" has come under criticism. In 2016, John Ellison, dean of the College at the University of Chicago, issued a welcome letter to the class of 2020, asserting the commitment to "academic freedom" requires the University "do[es] not condone the creation of intellectual 'safe spaces' where individuals can retreat from ideas and perspectives at odds with their own" (Ellison, 2016).

Ho (2017, Apr. 9) contends that rather than promoting dialogue, "safe spaces" lead to self-censoring for fear that "one small misstep will result in being on the receiving end of the "safe space" shaming bludgeon that is so prominently broadcast nationwide." A 2018 survey by the Pew Research Center indicates that among Republicans and Democrats who hold the view that "higher-education is going in the wrong direction," 79 percent and 31 percent, respectively, indicate colleges have "too much concern" about protecting students from views they might find offensive as a reason (Brown, 2018).

This chapter begins with a brief introduction to the relationship between "safe spaces" and classrooms promoting equity, diversity, and inclusion (EDI). It then turns to a summary of recent data on student attitudes regarding speech on campus and the need to help students differentiate from speech that silences and speech that challenges. The chapter then explores considerations and recommendations for instructors to establish and manage maximally inclusive dialogue in their classrooms with the aim of promoting social justice, equity, diversity, and inclusion (SJ-EDI) course outcomes while remaining respectful of student boundaries.

Courses containing social justice (SJ) and/or EDI components set cognitive, reflective, and affective learning outcomes for students around issues that may not be considered "safe." For example, SJ-EDI courses aim to increase students' self-awareness of their positionality within hierarchical social institutions, often culminating in an action-component promoting greater social equity and empathy. These transformative learning opportunities can create emotional discomfort (Adams, 2016; Hartwell et al., 2017).

For another example, SJ-EDI instructors deploy pedagogical philosophies and methodologies that challenge common student assumptions regarding the neutrality of knowledge, as well as the role of faculty and students as possessors and creators of knowledge (Adams, 2016; Hartwell et al., 2017). This can result in social anxiety and personal discomfort for participants and instructors. Therefore, instructors must work to create a classroom community within which all participants feel "safe" to share personal experiences and perspectives.

However, given current criticisms and misunderstandings surrounding curricular "safe spaces," instructors cannot presume students know what a "safe space" implies. Instructors should remain cognizant of shifting student attitudes toward potentially controversial speech in the classroom. Additionally, instructors need to articulate clearly that a curricular safe space does not limit *what can be said* but rather encourages reflection and empathy with regards to *how something is said.*

Most importantly, instructors declaring their classroom a "safe space" does not necessarily make it so. Each student is the judge as to whether their classroom space is "safe" for them to express their personal experiences and perspectives.

RECENT STUDENT ATTITUDES
TOWARD SPEECH ON CAMPUS

Recent surveys assessing student attitudes toward free speech on campus present a conflicted and murky landscape for instructors to navigate. Results of a 2017 survey of 1,250 undergraduates conducted by YouGov.com, published by The Foundation for Individual Rights in Education (FIRE), indicate that while 87 percent of students felt comfortable sharing opinions and ideas in the classroom, 54 percent indicated they had self-censored in the classroom, with 30 percent indicating they had self-censored for fear their viewpoint would be considered "offensive" to other students.

Additionally, a 2017 McLaughlin and Associates survey of 800 undergraduate students reveals significant disparities along political affiliation, with 61 percent of Republican-identifying students reporting they have "often felt intimidated sharing a belief that differed from their professor" compared to only 37 percent of Democratic-identifying students (McLaughlin and Associates, 2017). Finally, FIRE's 2018 survey indicated 81 percent of students agreed with the statement, "Words can be a form of violence." Despite this, however, only 38 percent of students favor having "speech codes" on their campuses (McLaughlin and Associates, 2017).

Selingo (2018) argues opportunities should exist at the curricular and co-curricular levels for students to practice differentiating speech with the intent to intimidate and silence others from speech with the intent to express or challenge a viewpoint. Courses with SJ-EDI components should provide ample opportunity for students to practice this skill.

Selingo also endorses recommendations issued in a 2018 report[1] published by ITHAKA S+R. They recommend the development of curriculum emphasizing the philosophic and historical importance of free speech, while developing robust antidiscrimination and anti-harassment policies (Hill et al., 2018). Additionally, SJ-EDI courses require institutional support so that students and instructors are confident the institutional culture supports SJ-EDI outcomes, activities, and instructional pedagogy (Garran and Rasmussen, 2014).

ADDITIONAL ACTIONS

The remainder of the chapter presents three additional actions instructors can take early in the class to address "safety" in the classroom: differentiating between curricular and cocurricular spaces; positioning oneself; and safety and comfort in transformative learning.

Differentiate between Curricular and Cocurricular Spaces

As Ho (2017, Jan. 30) notes, "safe spaces" originally referred to extracurricular groups organized to establish and maintain validating communities for historically marginalized students. Such spaces facilitate vital conversations within specific communities that in-group members might only feel comfortable having privately among themselves.

In the LGBTQ+ community, "safe spaces" or "safe zones" have historically functioned to identify campus administrators, faculty, and staff trained in LGBTQ+ literacy and issues and who have committed visibly, through the posting of a sticker, to be a validating and knowledgeable resource for LGBTQ+-identifying students. As Ho notes, "few would dispute the importance of these emotional spaces on campus" (2017, Jan. 30).

Notably, these safe spaces invite the question: Safe for who? The presence of a "Safe Zone" sticker on instructors' office doors signals their intention to be a "safe" person for an LGBTQ+-identifying student. It does not necessarily make instructors a safe or knowledgeable resource for students of other marginalized communities. Extracurricular "safe spaces" are typically established expressly to serve only a single community, and for that reason, they cannot—by design—incorporate the diversity of identity and viewpoints a curricular space must.

To address this potential confusion, instructors can alert their students on the first day of class that while they have a Safe Zone sticker posted on their office doors, that sticker is not posted on their classroom doors. In this way, instructors make explicit their self-awareness that their office Safe Zone sticker means that they are safe for a particular group—for example, "safe for LGBTQ+-identifying students"—and does not necessarily mean "safe for everyone." By contrast, the classroom space must be maximally safe for everyone—all identities and all viewpoints.

Position Oneself

Forty-four percent of students indicated they felt uncomfortable sharing their ideas and opinions in class because they were different from their professor's views (McLaughlin and Associates, 2017). Garran and Rasmussen (2014) note that the identity of the instructor plays a pivotal role in shaping student expectations about what "safety" will mean. Faculty should be aware that students might have preconceived assumptions about their viewpoints based on identity.

Moreover, faculty who teach content in which students perceive they have a personal investment must navigate difficult questions regarding the degree and type of personal disclosure and its impact on cultivating student trust that opposing viewpoints will be welcomed (Miller and Lucal, 2009). Faculty need to be reflective about their own positionality within the social institution of the classroom and model that reflection, at a minimum, by acknowledging their privileged role as instructor, regardless of their other non-privileged identities.

Safety and Comfort in Transformative learning

Adams (2016) provides a graphic model to articulate the relationship and difference between safety and comfort. She represents a student's comfort zone by a circle, with an individual's learning periphery situated at the edge of the circle, thereby placing the learning periphery outside of one's comfort zone but not so far outside as to be completely unassimilable. Arguably, information situated beyond the learning periphery could feel too threatening, leading to resistance.

Thus, Adams (2016) recommends that SJ-EDI activities aim for the learning periphery, the point at which the student experiences a level of discomfort where the information is potentially transformative but not so uncomfortable as to feel unsafe.

In addition, Concepción and Elfin (2009) provide a taxonomy of learning helpful for conceptualizing the degree of discomfort or distress new information occasions. They first differentiate between "additive" and "evaluative" learning. With additive learning, the student experiences the new information as "cohering with [their] preexisting beliefs and values"; with evaluative learning, the student experiences the new information as "incoherent . . . or to be in conflict" with their preexisting beliefs and values.

Evaluative learning is then further analyzed into "confirmative "and "transformative" learning. In confirmative learning, the student considers the new information but rejects it in favor of their preexisting beliefs and values. In transformative learning, the student revises salient elements of their preexisting beliefs and values so as to resolve the incoherence.

SJ-EDI courses encourage "evaluative" learning; participants frequently present and share information situated outside of any given student's "comfort zone," the zone of additive learning. However, Concepción and Elfin raise several critical cautions concerning evaluative learning. First, if a student considers the new information but does not revise their preexisting beliefs and values, this should not be taken as a refusal to learn. Evaluation of the new information in light of conflicting beliefs and values has occurred. Second, Concepción and Elfin contend that to the extent that transformative learning occurs, "unlearning" occurs.

In other words, in transformative learning, students reject prior beliefs and/or values they once held. Finally, transformative learning may require students to "unlearn" prior beliefs and/or values central to their identity, their sense of self-worth, and/or their sense of belonging in familial, cultural, or peer groups. Arguably, the degree to which new information conflicts with preexistent beliefs and values in which students are deeply invested personally or socially is the degree to which students have been asked to venture beyond their comfort zone.

Thus, to "aim at the periphery" of a student's comfort zone, participants must have some sense of each other's comfort zone. Hartwell et al. (2017) recommend that SJ-EDI courses open with exercises and activities that promote students' self-awareness (e.g., writing a brief autobiography). Such assignments provide opportunities for, at minimum, the instructor but also ideally other students, not merely to learn *what* other participants believe and value but also some of the *why* and *how* they came to hold these beliefs and values.

Moreover, as Garran and Rasmussen (2014) argue, students in nondominant positions regarding the salient social institutions and students in dominant positions with respect to those same institutions bring distinct concerns regarding the "safety" of a classroom space. Garran and Rasmussen note that students in dominant positions frequently fear "saying the wrong thing," "offending someone," and experiencing social and/or academic reprisal as a consequence, such as, for example, being labeled "racist," "sexist," and so on. Students in nondominant positions frequently fear being tokenized, invalidated, or tone-policed.

Of course, which students occupy dominant/nondominant positions is highly contextual and may include factors beyond the material or topic under consideration, including, but not limited to, the demographics of the participants—particularly the identity of the instructor (Garran and Rasmussen, 2014). Further, participants may disagree with the self-assessment of any particular individual regarding their positionality with respect to any given social institution, as well as within the classroom itself.

Thus, Garran and Rasmussen (2014) conclude that "classroom safety is not a singular concept, but rather a differentially experienced phenomenon that is related to questions embedded in power and privilege." Arguably, then, instructors face a delicate minimum/maximum problem adjudicating among and within students' preexistent beliefs and values, and their sense that given those beliefs and values, they are "safe" to engage with the materials, instructor(s), and the other students.

Safety and Comfort: An Analogy

Particularly for students associating speech with bullying and violence, instructors cannot assume students cognitively understand the difference between safety and comfort. Using the graphic model provided by Adams (2016) discussed in this chapter provides a simple way of illustrating that difference. However, even if students possess cognitive awareness of the distinction, it does not guarantee students will be capable of differentiating them in all circumstances.

Instructors should make explicit not merely the difference between safety and comfort, but they should also acknowledge that differentiating the two is a learned skill requiring frequent practice and nuanced self-awareness. As a long-time, frequent participant of group fitness classes and former instructor (indoor cycling), group physical fitness classes provide a helpful analogy to articulate both principles to students.

Just as college courses have unique learning outcomes, specific group fitness classes have specific fitness objectives: strength, cardiovascular health, endurance, and flexibility. Participants come to these classes with common general goals, but also specific personal goals: to lose weight, build muscle mass, and/or run a 5K. The value of group fitness is that not only the instructor but also the other students challenge and inspire each other to push harder than they might otherwise if exercising alone.

However, to achieve both these general and specific goals, participants must be willing to experience discomfort; just as one cannot achieve one's fitness goals without experiencing discomfort, so one cannot achieve one's learning goals without experiencing discomfort. The instructor's training should ensure all students remain safe. Instructors prioritize safety since any chronic or acute injury significantly jeopardizes the achievement of any fitness goals. The pedagogical implication here prioritizes students' own self-assessment of their safety regarding any specific classroom activity.

Participants bring to group fitness classes a wide range of abilities and experience, as well as health and injury history. Therefore, at the beginning of each class, a seasoned group-fitness instructor will ask participants if it is their first or second time in the class and if they have any injuries or health conditions. For inexperienced, injured, or pregnant participants, instructors offer modifications for certain exercises that, though safe for the general participant, are not safe for that particular individual. Modifications do not change the fitness goals of the class for those participants.

Modifications simply ensure that given one's injury and health history, the student can make progress toward their fitness goals without undue risk of chronic or acute injury. The pedagogical implication here stresses the need for differentiated instruction.

Finally, inexperienced participants might not reliably know when their discomfort is healthy or when it signals a potential injury or unsafe condition. This requires both self-reflection and experience. To illustrate this point, faculty should consider narrating a situation in which they navigated between an unsafe condition and discomfort.

As a personal example, recently, a group of students had a conversation outside this author's office. One student excoriated trans persons for several minutes while two students challenged this student's views. Overhearing this conversation as a trans person, this author felt extremely uncomfortable. However, they understood that despite their discomfort, as a tenured faculty member, they were not "unsafe."

This example aims to model for students both personal vulnerability and illustrates that discomfort does not always signal a lack of safety. Additionally, the narrative acknowledges the fluidity of dominant and nondominant positionality addressed by Garran and Rasmussen (2014): that as trans, the author occupies an unprivileged position regarding the cis student, with regards to the author's status as a tenured professor, they hold a privileged position with regards to the very same student.

CONCLUSION

Maintaining a safe and productive learning environment for SJ-EDI requires continual reinforcement and modeling (Adams, 2016). Established guidelines for interpersonal interactions and classroom behavior should be revisited and revised, if necessary. Students ought to be reminded of their own role in maintaining a safe and productive learning environment.

Though faculty may feel defensive or skeptical about a student requesting accommodation on the grounds that they feel "unsafe," faculty should validate the student's concerns while striving to make available modifications to assignments and activities that still work toward stated course learning outcomes. Despite all efforts to create a safe learning community, students ought to be reassured that they are the judge as to whether a learning community or discussion topic is "safe" for them.

NOTE

1. The Bowen Colloquium on Higher Education Leadership.

REFERENCES

Adams, M. (2016). Pedagogical foundations for social justice education. In M. Adams, L. A. Bell, D. J. Goodman, and K. Y. Joshi (Eds.), *Teaching for Diversity and Social Justice* (pp. 27–53). New York: Routledge.

Brown, A. (2018, July 26). Most Americans say higher ed. is heading in the wrong direction, but partisans disagree on why. *Pew Research Center*. Retrieved from http://www.pewresearch.org/fact-tank/2018/07/26/most-americans-say-higher-ed-is-heading-in-wrong-direction-but-partisans-disagree-on-why/.

Concepción, D. W., and Elfin, J. T. (2009). Enabling change: Transformative and transgressive learning in feminist ethics and epistemology. *Teaching Philosophy*, 32(2), 177–98.

Ellison, J. (2016). *Letter to class of 2020*. Retrieved from https://news.uchicago.edu/sites/default/files/attachments/Dear_Class_of_2020_Students.pdf.

Foundation for Individual Rights in Education. (2017). *Student attitudes free speech survey*. Retrieved from https://www.thefire.org/publications/student-surveys/student-attitudes-free-speech-survey/student-attitudes-free-speech-survey-full-text/.

Foundation for Individual Rights in Education. (2018). *Student attitudes association survey*. Retrieved from https://www.thefire.org/publications/student-surveys/student-attitudes-association-survey/student-attitudes-association-survey-full-text/.

Garran, A. M., and Rasmussen, B. M. (2014). Safety in the classroom: Reconsidered. *Journal of Teaching in Social Work* 34, 401–12. doi:10.1080/08841233.2014.937 517.

Hartwell, E., et al. (2017). Breaking down silos: Teaching for equity, diversity, and inclusion across disciplines. *Humboldt Journal for Social Relations*, 1(39), 143–62.

Hill, C. B., et al. (2018, Feb. 28). Free speech, student activism and social media: Reflections from the Bowen Colloquium on higher education leadership. *ITHAKA S+R*. Retrieved from https://sr.ithaka.org/wp-content/uploads/2018/02/SR-Report-Bowen-Colloquium-Free-Speech-02282018.pdf.

Ho, K. (2017, Jan. 30). Tackling the term: What is a safe space? *Harvard Political Review*. Retrieved from http://harvardpolitics.com/harvard/what-is-a-safe-space/.

Ho, K. (2017, Apr. 9). Defending a culture of free speech. *Harvard Political Review*. Retrieved from http://harvardpolitics.com/harvard/defending-culture-free-speech/.

McLaughlin and Associates. (2017, Sept. 28). *National undergraduate survey*. Retrieved from http://c8.nrostatic.com/sites/default/files/NATL%20Undergrad%209-27-17%20Presentation%20%281%29.pdf.

Miller, A., and Lucal, B. (2009). The pedagogy of (in)visibility: two accounts of teaching about sex, gender, and sexuality. *Teaching Sociology*, 37(3), 257–68.

Selingo, J. J. (2018). The new generation of students: How colleges can recruit, teach and serve Gen Z. *The Chronicle of Higher Education*. Retrieved from http://connect.chronicle.com/rs/931-EKA-218/images/NextGenStudents_Executive Summary_v5%20_2019.pdf.

About the Authors

Chris Adamo (they/their) serves as associate professor of philosophy at Centenary University where they teach courses in the humanities. They have published on the intersection of political liberalism and utopian literature. They have spoken on supporting trans/GNC (gender nonconforming) children and conducted Safe Zone training sessions.

Kim Barber is a business professional with an academic passion. She is an advocate for students, and her passion and commitment has focused on increasing diversity and closing the achievement gap. Dr. Barber was appointed to both the Diversity Committee and the Strategic Planning Committee for The Council for Postsecondary Education in the state of Kentucky.

Amy Bergstrom is an associate professor in The School of Education at The College of St. Scholastica, where she serves as the director of the master of education degree program. Dr. Bergstrom teaches graduate courses in the areas of EDI, serves on the inclusive excellence college-wide task force, and is an enrolled member of the Red Lake Band of Chippewa in Northern Minnesota.

Betsy Bowen is a professor of English and faculty chair of service learning at Fairfield University, where she teaches courses on literacy, writing, and children's literature. She was selected as 2010 Connecticut Professor of the Year by the Carnegie Foundation for the Advancement of Teaching and was recognized by the Connecticut Department of Higher Education for community service.

Stephanie L. Burrell Storms is an associate dean and associate professor of multicultural education at Fairfield University. Her teaching and scholarly interests include social justice education, scholarship of teaching and learning (SoTL), and faculty development. Stephanie is the Region 1 Director for the National Association for Multicultural Education.

Kyle Forrest is a cognitive psychologist and psychotherapist who has worked in academia and private practice for over fifteen years. Kyle is a senior lecturer at the University of Washington, Tacoma, and an executive coach for lawyers. He has a focus on trauma, shame, and anti-oppressive pedagogies.

Samira Garcia is a faculty member at Valdosta State University's master of science in marriage and family therapy program and a licensed marriage and family therapist. Her research examines the conversational processes of utilizing postmodern, constructivist psychotherapy models in working with couples.

Paula Gill Lopez is chair of the Department of Psychological and Educational Consultation and director of school psychology in the Graduate School of Education and Allied Professions at Fairfield University. She has been practicing mindfulness since 2008.

Kevin Hermberg is a professor of philosophy and chair of the general education curriculum at Dominican College. He is cofounder and editor of the Bloomsbury series *Issues in Phenomenology and Hermeneutics* and co-editor in chief of *AAPT Studies in Pedagogy*.

Carla Hilario is an assistant professor in the faculty of nursing at the University of Alberta. Dr. Hilario currently teaches graduate and undergraduate courses in health promotion and Indigenous health. Her research focuses on mental health promotion and equity-oriented, youth-engaged research.

Hyun Uk Kim has taught and trained prospective special education teachers since 2007, most recently at Simmons College. Dr. Kim strives to empower prospective educators to create a society with the least restrictive attitudes toward disability and special education.

Rory E. Kraft Jr. is an assistant professor of philosophy and chair of the Department of English, Humanities, and the Arts at York College. He is editor emeritus of *Questions: Philosophy for Young People* and co-editor in chief of *AAPT Studies in Pedagogy*. His areas of research are ethics (theory and applied), philosophy with children, and aesthetics.

Tabitha McCoy, LMFT, is the clinic manager and internship supervisor for the Marriage and Family Therapy Program at Valdosta State University. Both her clinical and research interests focus on working with military families through various stages of transition, walk-in, single-session therapy with diverse populations, as well as best practices for training master's level and postgraduate students.

Danica Sterud Miller (Puyallup Tribe of Indians) grew up on one of the last allotments of the Puyallup reservation. She teaches American Indian studies at the University of Washington, Tacoma, which is located on her ancestral homelands. Her research focuses on her twinned obsessions of Puyallup history and Lushootseed language revitalization.

Stephaney Morrison is an assistant professor of counselor education in the Graduate School of Education and Allied Professions at Fairfield University. Dr. Morrison's research focuses on training school counselors to work with immigrant families and children, which has garnered several published articles and book chapters.

Hoa Nguyen is an assistant professor in the Marriage and Family Therapy Program at Valdosta State University. She teaches courses on diversity, inclusion, and social justice, queering family therapy practices, and cultivating dialogue across differences. Her area of research focuses on the migration narratives of lesbian, gay, bisexual, and queer individuals.

Kathi Rainville is a teacher librarian in a K-3 school in Bethel, Connecticut. With a prior career in broadcasting, she continues her freelance voice-over work and enjoys reading and recording children's books using different character voices. As a teacher, Kathi enjoys engaging students with literature and learning about their world.

Jay Rozgonyi is the associate vice provost for pedagogical innovation and effectiveness at Fairfield University, as well as a faculty member in the educational technology program. A frequent presenter at both regional and national workshops and conferences, Jay was named one of 2015's Top 30 Technologists, Transformers, and Trailblazers by the Center for Digital Education.

Peter Thompson is a psychologist who has worked with individuals and groups for more than forty years. Peter has been an adjunct clinical instructor at the University of Washington, was founder and codirector of the Gestalt

Institute of Seattle, and was formerly an Episcopal priest. He has a background in trauma, addiction, and organizational shame.

Josephine Wong is a professor at the Daphne Cockwell School of Nursing at Ryerson University. Dr. Wong's teaching focuses on community health nursing and people-centered health promotion with an emphasis on social justice and health equity. Her research is underpinned by the principle of doing research "with" and "not for" the affected communities.

CPSIA information can be obtained
at www.ICGtesting.com
Printed in the USA
BVHW031652100320
574630BV00001B/16

9 781475 843392